SceneWriting

Diana Wynne

SceneWriting

The Missing Manual for Screenwriters

Chris Perry and
Eric Henry Sanders

BLOOMSBURY ACADEMIC
NEW YORK • LONDON • OXFORD • NEW DELHI • SYDNEY

BLOOMSBURY ACADEMIC
Bloomsbury Publishing Inc
1385 Broadway, New York, NY 10018, USA
50 Bedford Square, London, WC1B 3DP, UK
29 Earlsfort Terrace, Dublin 2, Ireland

BLOOMSBURY, BLOOMSBURY ACADEMIC and the Diana logo are trademarks of
Bloomsbury Publishing Plc

First published in the United States of America 2022

For legal purposes the Acknowledgments on p. 241 constitute an extension of this
copyright page.

Cover design: Eleanor Rose
Cover images: Spotlight © Getty Images; Screenplay courtesy of the authors.

Library of Congress Cataloging-in-Publication Data
Names: Perry, Chris, 1970- author. | Sanders, Eric Henry, author.
Title: Scenewriting : the missing manual for screenwriters /
Chris Perry and Eric Henry Sanders.
Description: New York : Bloomsbury Academic, 2022. | Includes bibliographical
references and index. | Summary: "The first comprehensive guide to mastering the art
and craft of writing scenes, providing screenwriters with a new foundational approach
to creating beautifully articulated scripts"– Provided by publisher.
Identifiers: LCCN 2021047857 (print) | LCCN 2021047858 (ebook) |
ISBN 9781501352133 (hardback) | ISBN 9781501352126 (paperback) |
ISBN 9781501352140 (epub) | ISBN 9781501352157 (pdf)
Subjects: LCSH: Motion picture authorship. | Motion picture plays–Technique.
Classification: LCC PN1996 .P467 2022 (print) | LCC PN1996 (ebook) |
DDC 808.2/3—dc23/eng/20211027
LC record available at https://lccn.loc.gov/2021047857
LC ebook record available at https://lccn.loc.gov/2021047858

ISBN: HB: 978-1-5013-5213-3
        PB: 978-1-5013-5212-6
        ePDF: 978-1-5013-5215-7
        eBook: 978-1-5013-5214-0

Typeset by RefineCatch Limited, Bungay, Suffolk

To find out more about our authors and books visit www.bloomsbury.com
and sign up for our newsletters.

To our students and teachers

Contents

Part III **Perfecting** 139

9 **Check Your Length** 141

10 **Managing Scene Information in Dialogue** 153

11 **Bringing Authenticity into Your Dialogue** 169

Why a Book about Scenes?

Oh shoot, now you've done it. You opened the book.

Listen, there's still time to change your mind. Because after you've read *SceneWriting*, you'll never be able to look at storytelling the same way. You won't be able to glance at a script or watch shows and movies in blissful simplicity ever again. Instead, you'll know how they work, how their stories were crafted, how the magic was created line by line. And once that genie is out of the bottle, you can never pop it back in.

Even more importantly, reading this book is going to complicate your dreams of being a successful screenwriter. You know that fantasy, that a brilliant script is about a good idea and a caffeine-induced writing binge? It's just not true. This book, instead, will show you how to develop your craft. And that takes work. Attention. Thought. Diligence. Revision.

This is your last chance. Knowledge or ignorance? You can still put the book down. Reshelve it, walk away, and live easy.

Okay! We admire your pluck.

Here's the deal:

Through our years of teaching, young writers have come to us full of passion, wild ideas, and unique perspectives on the world. When they hit the screenwriting literature, they begin to gain knowledge of multi-act structures, loglines, the hero's journey, genre tropes, beat outlines, season-wide arcs, act breaks, and the like. These are incredibly useful ideas and wonderful tools, but they're all about the big picture.

But brilliant scripts are more than just well-structured outlines. They are a progression of indelible *scenes* that engage readers through a blend of dialogue, action, and setting. And that's where *SceneWriting* comes in. Unlike other texts, we walk you through the entire process of writing a fully realized scene from idea development to final delivery.

Planning, Drafting, Perfecting

We approach the *scenewriting* process by breaking it into three manageable parts:

Planning (Part I) is about making sure you have everything you need before you start putting words to the page. Characters. Obstacles. A setting. A time of day. A statement of theme. And an understanding of what you need the scene to accomplish in story terms. There's a truism that says *the hardest part of writing is knowing what to write*. Part I exists to ensure you know.

Drafting (Part II) is where you will dash out the first version of your scene in all its clumsy glory. Here you will translate the story ideas that you developed in Part I into engaging dialogue and scene description. You'll learn about sluglines, ALLCAPS, "wrylies," and other curiosities of the screenplay format. You'll produce the first full draft of your scene, celebrate briefly, and then turn to the final stage of the process.

Perfecting (Part III) is where you will learn the truth of the expression that "writing is rewriting." You will become a master of subtext, an assassin of redundant exposition, and a crafter of tone. You will learn how to breathe compelling naturalism into dialogue, make your scene description evocative and efficient, and deliver a beautiful page. Part III is dedicated to polishing your scene into a brilliant final product, suitable for sharing with the rest of us who are desperate to read it.

We wouldn't want to imply that we think there's only one way to write, and that it's ours. After all, successful screenwriters everywhere have figured out how to do it even without this book (shocking!). But what we offer is a comprehensive and effective method developed over decades of teaching that will help you write great scenes. And it works.

The idea is this: You will pick a scene to develop using the book as a guide. It doesn't matter if your scene is a one-scene short film or if it's pulled from the beat outline of a larger feature or series project. Any scene will do.

By working through the book, you'll bring your scene to life bit-by-bit with the exercises that appear at the end of every section. The exercises are straightforward and instructional. They will help you to develop your scene one easy step at a time.

Each chapter will expose you to a ton of new tools and writing techniques. Take what you find useful into your madly successful future.

What is a Great Scene, Anyway?

Let's get on the same page about this right away.

By our definition, a great scene is a contained portion of a script that accomplishes three things:

First, a great scene *provides new story information* to the reader. This information might relate to a character's goal, their motivation, an obstacle in their way, and/or their particular approach to overcoming that obstacle. Put another way, new story information relates to questions such as: What do characters want? Why do they want it? What's stopping them from getting it? And, what are they going to do about it?

Second, a great scene must *resolve* and signal what comes next. The resolution brings to a close the action of the scene, and the signal compels your readers to continue on your characters' journey.

Finally, a great scene must actively *engage the reader* in experiencing the story. Without engagement, you've written an instruction manual. Reader engagement can be intellectual or emotional or both. And the more engagement, the better.

Information. Resolution. Engagement. That's it.

The goal of this book is to help you write a scene that delivers in all three of these critical areas. We'll get you there by walking you through a process of planning, drafting, and perfecting that you can consistently and reliably repeat with any of your subsequent scenes.

So, if you're looking for guidance on how to translate your well-structured story into a riveting script, one great scene at a time, then look no further.

Welcome to *SceneWriting*—glad you kept reading.

PART I

Planning

You're probably dying to write FADE IN. You imagine yourself tapping away at a keyboard, coffee steaming in a mug beside you, a pensive glow sparkling in your eyes as your characters spring to life on the page. It's a nice image. And it will happen. But not until you know what you're doing with the words that come after FADE IN.

That's where planning comes in.

"No!" you protest, "Not *planning*! I'm an artist, a free spirit, a wild pony."

To which we say, just hear us out. What typically happens to writers who don't plan is that they crank out page after page of disconnected dialogue and deadening scene description. It doesn't engage. It doesn't cohere.

And they can see it, right there on the page: it's awful. This realization can make a person hate writing and do something drastic like go pre-med. Which is, you know, pretty good for humanity and everything, but it's no way to end a screenwriting career.

So first you've got to figure out what you want to write. By following the ideas and exercises discussed in this first part of this book, *Planning*, you will translate the passion and excitement you have into exactly what you need to write your scene.

Over the next four chapters you will pin down what your characters want, why, and what obstacles are in their way. You'll identify the unique approach that your characters take in an effort to overcome them. You will also figure out where and when your scene takes place and how to end it so that your readers can't wait to read more. Finally, you'll articulate your tone and theme and weave the events of your scene around both.

In short, if you have a good plan going in, then all your work will naturally flow into a unified design. So forge ahead, and lay the foundation for your great scene.

1 What Do They Want and Why?

People pursuing their desires—going after goals they want to attain—is what changes the world. And the same is true in stories. It doesn't matter if you're writing a feature, a series, or a short film: your character's pursuit of a goal is what prompts them to act.

This is true for your scene as well. Whatever scene you choose to develop in this book (you'll choose one shortly) will be driven forward by your character acting on their desire. In that way, it will be an awesome little version of your character's larger tale.

Setting a goal for your main character gives direction to the journey. It leads your reader towards a destination. It's also the first step in setting up lots of questions to engage the reader's interest: will the character get what they're after? How will they succeed or fail?

Nothing strikes fear in our hearts quite like a student saying that their main character doesn't want anything: "My character is just really confused and isn't sure what they're doing." Without a clear character desire, we know we'll be wandering aimless around the frozen steppes of their seriously boring script.

So this is why we start with desire.

What's It All about?

When asked what a story is "about," you may hear answers like the following:

> THE LORD OF THE RINGS: A sheltered hobbit must travel to Mordor to destroy the Ring of Power before the enemy gets it and takes over the world.

CASABLANCA: A heartbroken bar owner tries to stay out of the war but is pulled into it by his lost love.

SELMA: A non-violent, activist preacher wants to secure equal voting rights but comes up against the deadly and terrifying face of systemic racism in the deep south.

BOOKSMART: Two overachieving best friends want to experience a high school party before they graduate.

Story summaries like these really highlight the importance of character desire: A character wants something, they set out to pursue it, and the story chronicles their journey towards what they want.

We call these kinds of summaries "plot-centric" because they focus on the characters, what they want, what they do, who they encounter, and in general are concerned with what you might call story facts.

There is another completely different way of answering the question of what a story is "about." Stories are also about things like:

THE LORD OF THE RINGS: Absolute power can corrupt even the purest mind.

CASABLANCA: Sometimes you have to do what's right, no matter the cost.

SELMA: Non-violent resistance is a force for change.

BOOKSMART: There's more than one way to succeed in high school (and life).

These summaries speak to the *themes* of stories instead of their plots. They are not about the facts, per se. Instead, they look to the overall messages and speak of them in allegorical terms. We call these "theme-centric" summaries.

Chances are you've come to your story idea by one of these two routes. For example: Perhaps you can't wait to write a story about a woman searching all over New York City for her lost cat (plot-centric). Or maybe you're just dying to write a story about the corrupting nature of money (theme-centric).

Regardless of how you got here, we're going to focus on helping you figure out the plot side of things first. The reason for starting with plot is because it's much easier to see how theme emerges from plot than the other way around.

For example: let's say you work out the plot details of the story about the woman searching for her cat, and in the end (after an exhaustive journey all over town) she finds that the cat's been asleep under her bed at home the whole time. The theme of this story based on these plot details is probably something like, "we already have the things we seek, we just have to realize it."

But imagine doing things the other way. Let's say you want to write a story with the message of "we already have the things we seek, we just have to realize it." That doesn't inherently suggest a woman looking for her lost cat all over New York City, does it? Indeed, you could cook up countless plots that speak to this same theme. Like THE WIZARD OF OZ, ISN'T IT ROMANTIC, SULLIVAN'S TRAVELS, and THE SURE THING, to name a few.

In other words, a specific plot is likely to suggest a specific theme, but not the other way around. So let's start with plot. But don't worry, we will return to theme a lot, because you ultimately will write your scene with both in mind.

The plot-centric version of your story is driven by what we call your character's *overarching goal*. This is the goal that drives the events of your longer story and is the one that, when concluded, signals the end of the film or series to the audience. The overarching goal allows your reader to know in what direction the longer work is heading.

> Dorothy wanting to return home to Kansas in THE WIZARD OF OZ, Brody wanting to kill the shark in JAWS, and Harry wanting to be with Sally in WHEN HARRY MET SALLY are some examples of overarching goals.

EXERCISE: Overarching Goal

Start a new empty document for yourself that you can return to as you complete the exercises throughout this book. It could be a digital file on your computer or a simple notebook.

If you've come to this book because you're working on a larger story, like a feature or a pilot, then:

Write down the name of your main character.

Write down what your main character wants to achieve as their overarching goal in your story. This might not have coalesced for you, yet, into the specificity of "Luke Skywalker wants to blow up the Death Star," but it will. For now it's okay to be more general, like, "Luke Skywalker wants to defeat the Evil Empire." Jot down what you have so far, even if it is no more specific than "triumph over evil," "fall in love," or "solve the crime."

Look for an overarching goal that once achieved (or lost irrevocably) will conclude your story. Don't worry too much about making it perfect. At this point in the writing process you are simply giving yourself a beacon to row towards. The goal will evolve as you write your scene(s) and it will definitely become clearer as you make progress on your script.

If you don't have a larger story in the works:

That's okay! Skip this exercise. In the next one, you can pick a scene to develop using this book and still learn everything we have to teach you.

One Does Not Simply Walk Into Mordor

Overarching goals are too involved to accomplish in one action, so writers break the challenge into smaller *scene goals* for their characters to pursue.

In a scene from RAIDERS OF THE LOST ARK, Indiana Jones wants to get the headpiece of the Staff of Ra from his deceased mentor's daughter, Marion. That is his scene goal. Jones's need for the headpiece, however, is in service of his overarching goal: to recover the Ark of the Covenant before his Nazi competitor gets it.

In a scene from LITTLE MISS SUNSHINE, Richard wants to sneak Grandpa's dead body out of the hospital. That's his scene goal. It's a step towards accomplishing his overarching goal of getting Olive to the Little Miss Sunshine pageant on time.

In a scene from EIGHTH GRADE, Kayla wants to have a private conversation with her crush during a lockdown drill in class. That's her scene goal. But why she wants to have that conversation is because her overarching goal is to become the ideal eighth grader she thinks she is supposed to be (which includes having a popular boyfriend).

Your scene will work in the same way. In it, your character will pursue a scene goal that is a stepping stone towards the completion of some larger overarching goal.

Kinds of Scene Goals

So, what exactly is a scene goal? The short answer is that it can be almost anything that a character wants. This might sound infinite—and we encourage you to be as creative as you like—but to narrow things a bit, there are four broad possibilities that appear again and again in scenes. They are:

Objects

Does my character want to get—or give up—a specific object? It could be something as mundane as the last bag of flour at the supermarket, the cookie that Ezra is eating, or a full tank of gas. Or it could be as uncommon as the key piece of evidence for the trial, a knife that an opponent is wielding, or the Sorcerer's Stone.

Words from Others

Does your character need to hear something specific from another character? Whether it's words of forgiveness, expressions of love, the code for the safe, an explicit promise, or a confession, characters always seem to want other people to tell them things. (Is that needy? It sounds needy.)

Getting Somewhere

People (and thus, characters) are always wanting to go places: they've got to get to the church on time, the emergency room, or the boat dock; they need to sneak inside the locked office building, get off to school, or meet that foreign agent in the gloomy parking lot at midnight; they want to escape from prison, get out of the haunted house, or make it safely back to earth after circling the moon in a busted lunar lander.

Completing a Task

Are they trying to complete a specific task? This can be as commonplace as renting a car, or as unusual as keeping a Balrog from killing your traveling companions.

Qualities of Scene Goals

Regardless of the specific scene goal that you choose for your character, in order to serve its critical function in advancing your story, your scene goal needs to be *relatable*, *specific*, and *achievable*.

But keep in mind that although you, the writer, must know everything about your character's scene goal, you might not share all those details with your reader right away. In other words, you absolutely could present your character taking actions with a purpose and motivation towards some goal that the reader doesn't fully grasp (yet). What you know, versus what you share, is the distinction between *story* and *storytelling*, a point we'll get to in great depth in Part II. For now, and throughout the rest of Part I, your goal is to get as clear as you can so that YOU know what you're writing.

Relatability

Let's say your character's scene goal is to buy a latte. The problem is, your scene is being read by a studio boss who hates coffee. Does that mean she won't like it?

Not at all. Because what matters more in this context is *why* your character wants that latte. Is the latte part of a morning ritual your character needs to jump start their day? Is it because they're going to dump it on the obnoxious guy talking on his cellphone in the corner? Is it because they're excited to flirt with the cute barista?

Even someone who hates coffee can relate to any of these very human impulses. This is what we mean by *relatable*. As long as you write your scene goal so that a relatable human impulse emerges, your reader will natively understand the *why* even if they've never shared the desire for that specific *what*.

> In EIGHTH GRADE, Kayla records a life-advice video. Even people who never wanted to have an audience on YouTube can easily relate to Kayla's wish to connect with others.

> In SPIDER-MAN: INTO THE SPIDERVERSE, Miles Morales returns to the subway tunnels trying to figure out why he suddenly has super-sticky hands. Even someone who has never braved the bowels of the NYC subway or been bitten by a radioactive spider can understand Miles wanting to figure out the source of the mysterious changes happening to him.

> In LITTLE MISS SUNSHINE, Olive rehearses a performance for the beauty contest. Whatever people might think of beauty contests, anyone can relate to wanting to compete and win.

Relatability is pretty simple because when it comes down to it, there isn't a ton of variation in basic human desires, even though there is infinite variation in how those desires are realized. As long as the reader understands the *why* behind your character's want, they will relate to your character and want to keep reading.

Specificity

Your character has to fix the spaceship engine. Are they looking for any old widget, or for the 6cm double-plated Oxytech spanner?

It's gotta be the spanner. *Specificity* is super helpful for both you and your reader. And we're talking super-specific like: "talk your way into an exclusive restaurant by posing as Abe Froman, the Sausage King of Chicago" or "steal the Chachapoyan Fertility Idol and escape the Peruvian temple alive" or "get Edna Mode to repair your torn supersuit." Knowing the details of your character's scene goal will help you to write a believable and convincing scene, even if that specificity isn't revealed until later.

An unemployed character, for example, might start a job hunt only knowing that they want "to find a job," or a character stranded in the wilderness might simply be desperate to "find something to eat." But as the scenewriter, you should be prepared to reveal the dog-walking gig, or the turtle eggs buried by the lake bed. (Turtle eggs? Gross, sure, but the guy is desperate.)

You must have a full understanding of the world of your story so that you can support it, even if you don't yet share all that information with your character and your reader. You'll hear a lot more about not sharing everything in Chapter 6.

Specificity helps the reader understand if the scene goal has been met or not. In other words, it allows your reader to track your character's progress in measurable terms. Does he pick the lock successfully at 168 Maple Road or not? Does she save the penalty kick or doesn't she? Do they get a spot on the lifeboat or not? Asking these kinds of scene questions will get your reader invested in your story. Here are a few more examples:

> In a scene from CAN YOU EVER FORGIVE ME?, Lee tries to sell a personal letter she received from Katharine Hepburn in order to make some cash. Will she or won't she succeed?

> In a scene from GET OUT, Chris wants to leave the uncomfortable late-night conversation with Missy, his girlfriend's mother, and go back to bed. Does he escape or is he drawn further into her web?

> In a scene from STAR WARS, Luke wants to catch up with his friends at Anchorhead, but his uncle insists that he must first clean the new droid, R2-D2. Will Luke get to Anchorhead or not?

Achievability

Contemporary scenes generally run in the two- to four-minute range, so it's important for any scene goal to be *achievable* within that limited time. This doesn't mean the goal *will* be achieved, nor does it mean that achieving it will be easy. It just has to be the case that the goal is possible to achieve within that limited time.

Achievability can be tricky to measure. After all, film is a magic medium. Through editing, a character in a movie can run a marathon in 30 seconds, or travel across the globe during one animated shot of a map. Thankfully, aside from extreme tonal and stylistic exceptions, scenes generally play out in real time. So the most helpful guide to constructing a good scene goal is: can your character either fail or succeed at this scene goal within three or fewer minutes? If the answer is no, then your goal is probably too big for one scene. If that's the case, reduce the scope.

The examples above regarding specificity are also perfect examples of achievability. Selling a letter and leaving a conversation are all achievable within the scope of a "few minutes' time." And although we don't necessarily know how long it takes to clean a droid, we get the impression from the scene that it's a chore like detailing a car or mowing the lawn. And just like that, it becomes achievable.

EXERCISE: And . . . Scene.

It's time to pick your scene!

This might feel like a momentous decision, but don't think too hard on it.

If you've been working on a larger story:

> Pick a scene that speaks to you. Maybe it's a scene that keeps coming to your mind when you imagine the finished piece, or maybe it's the scene that inspired you to write the story in the first place. If you don't have an obvious choice, pick one that feels easy and contained.

If you don't have a larger story, or don't want to work on yours quite yet:

> Cook up a single-scene short for the purposes of this book. Your whole scene in this case will be about someone trying to achieve their scene goal. And that's fine. Use the rest of this exercise to identify who it is and the details of what they want, and you'll have created the framework of a solid short scene even without a larger story.

Whatever you choose, you'll get more out of this experience if you're actually writing instead of skipping over the exercises. So really, any scene will do.

Now it's time to pin down the goal and desire that will drive your scene forward.

Adding specific details where you need them, copy down the following sentence but replace the allcaps with the details from your scene:

CHARACTER wants to SCENE GOAL.

For example:

Betty wants to go back into the dance club and retrieve the purse she forgot inside.

And:

Seventh-grader Kara wants to dance with Janelle at the middle-school formal.

And:

Detective Shovel wants to find a clue at the crime scene (it turns out to be the culprit's bloody thumbprint on a perfume bottle).

Notice that the third example would have lacked specificity if not for the parenthetical note. In this case, Shovel doesn't know what he's looking for (yet), but it's important that, as the writer, we make this clear to ourselves. By the way, you'll get to know Betty, Kara, Janelle, and Detective Shovel well because we return to their scenes throughout this book.

To make sure your character's scene goal is *relatable*, flesh out the following:

CHARACTER'S desire to achieve SCENE GOAL is relatable because everyone understands _____.

In our example cases:

Betty's desire to get her purse back is relatable because everyone understands what it's like to lose something.

And:

> Kara's desire to dance with Janelle is relatable because everyone
> understands having a crush and hoping to act on it.

And:

> Detective Shovel's desire to find a clue is relatable because everyone
> understands wanting to do a job well, wanting to solve a puzzle, and
> wanting to see justice done.

Finally, if your scene is part of a larger story, clarify how this scene is a stepping stone towards your character's overarching goal in that larger story. For example:

> Betty wants to live on her own. She's trying to convince her mom that
> she's responsible enough to do so, and showing up after curfew
> without her purse is going to be a huge step backwards in that larger
> quest.

If you don't see the connection between your character's scene goal and their overarching goal, then you might want to pick another scene.

That's it! Now you have an understanding of exactly what your character wants in your scene, and you've identified how your readers will relate to that desire.

2 Why Can't They Have It?

Even if your characters have wonderfully specific, relatable, and achievable goals, you won't have a story if they can get what they're after without a struggle.

If Ilsa walks into Rick's gin joint, they rush into each other's arms, and ten minutes later they're on a plane to New York, you've got no CASABLANCA. If a grandfather and grandson team can simply carry the Mega Seeds off Dimension 35-C without having to painfully smuggle them past intergalactic customs, you've lost the magic of RICK AND MORTY.

Obstacles are the things that stand between your character and their goals. By creating conflict, obstacles are integral to compelling stories.

If you can establish obstacles that are difficult, if not seemingly impossible, for your characters to knock down, your readers will thrill to the pleasure of watching them muddle, struggle, and claw their way through. In other words, there's an entire universe of possibilities, and it's up to you to choose the obstacle(s) that will make your characters' lives hell.

Fun. Where do you start?

The Universe Is out to Get You

You may have a dim recollection from middle school of lumping the different kinds of dramatic conflict into (anachronistic and patriarchal) categories like "man vs. man," "man vs. nature," and so on. We've consolidated and renamed these outdated groupings into the following:

Character vs. Other

Character vs. Thing

Character vs. Self

You Can't Share a Parking Space

The most prevalent obstacles your characters are likely to face are sentient *Others* that adapt and react to what your character does. An Other is anyone your character wants something from, friend or foe: Hannibal Lecter (SILENCE OF THE LAMBS), Katara (AVATAR: THE LAST AIRBENDER), Stringer Bell (THE WIRE), or Lisa Simpson (THE SIMPSONS). Pitting one character against an Other allows for a meeting of minds, a clashing of wits, or a showdown of goals and philosophies.

Most Others are human characters, but they need not be. They could be beasts (Smaug in THE HOBBIT), robots (The Terminator in THE TERMINATOR, Hal in 2001: A SPACE ODYSSEY, Ava in EX MACHINA), supernatural beings (The Snow Queen in THE CHRONICLES OF NARNIA: THE LION, THE WITCH AND THE WARDROBE, The Wicked Witch of the West in THE WIZARD OF OZ), aliens (Thanos in AVENGERS: INFINITY WAR), or really any other intelligent, adaptive opponent you can dream up.

In Character versus Other situations, your opposing character needs to have a *mutually exclusive goal* in order to create conflict; otherwise they aren't really obstructing your main character's quest.

For example: two characters are trying to park their cars. If there are plenty of spaces, then each character can easily get what they want because there's no obstacle. But if there's only one space available, then they both can't have what they want, so the stage is set for conflict. Note that parking a car is not even required here: if one character wants to play hopscotch in the contested space, then the conflict would still exist.

> In PEN15 (Season 1, Episode 9), Anna is sleeping over at Maya's house and wants them both to go play with Maya's brother. But Maya is excited to have Anna over and wants to play with her alone. They both can't have what they want.
>
> In THE PRINCESS BRIDE, the Dread Pirate Roberts and The Sicilian engage in a battle of wits over their contested captive, Princess Buttercup. Only one can win.
>
> In the pilot episode of THE WIRE, Detective McNulty wants a witness to identify who killed poor Snotboogie. But the witness

won't talk because he doesn't want to testify in court. These two mutually exclusive desires mean that one will win and one will lose.

Whenever you pit two characters against each other, keep in mind that power dynamics exist between them. Great battles can and do occur all the time between equally matched opponents (think game seven of the World Series, for example). But the victories are more unlikely, and therefore sweeter, when an underdog overcomes a great imbalance of power. David versus Goliath. Erin Brockovich versus PG&E. The Bears versus the Yankees in THE BAD NEWS BEARS.

Power dynamics are not as simple as "the stronger one wins." A parent struggling with a toddler in public may actually have less power because the toddler doesn't care at all what everyone in the restaurant thinks. The film MOUSEHUNT is full of scenes featuring a tiny rodent completely outclassing two grown men. Who has the power here?

But I Thought We Were Friends

Sometimes your character's allies will act in ways that oppose your character's scene goal and become obstacles themselves. Two friends might, for example, argue over the best way to defeat a dragon. In such a scene they are each other's obstacle.

Whether they begin the scene as a friend or not, if a character acts like an obstacle in your scene, then they're an obstacle. And friends can be the toughest obstacles! Because they know so much about your main character and generally share a similar set of values, it may seem as if the character is up against another side of themselves.

> In EIGHTH GRADE, Kayla catches her otherwise supportive and encouraging father spying on her at the mall with her new friends. His presence jeopardizes her chance of building these friendships.
>
> In GET OUT, Chris wants to go to his girlfriend's parents' house for the weekend, but his best friend tries to convince him it's a terrible idea (spoiler alert: he's right).

In MOONLIGHT, Chiron's friend and lover, Kevin, fights with him at school because he's pressured to by other classmates.

Lions and Tigers and Bears, Oh My!

If your character is stuck on one side of a river and the treasure they're after is on the other side, yelling at the river won't do much good. Building a makeshift raft, on the other hand, might do the trick. Hitching a ride on the back of a crossing water buffalo, phoning for an airlift, or fashioning a rope out of suspenders are all great options, depending upon the kind of script you're writing.

Rivers, as obstacles, are not intelligent. They don't react and adapt to things that happen to them. Our catchy term for these dumb roadblocks is "Things." Other examples include locked doors, zombies, tornadoes, minefields, giant blood-sucking leeches, and flesh-eating bacteria.

Talking won't help when confronted by a Thing. Instead, your character is going to have to do something physically crafty to get past them. Or run away.

In the opening scene of TOY STORY 2, Buzz Lightyear wants to find Zurg's fortress, but he's surrounded by hundreds of robots with lasers pointing at him.

In the film BRIDESMAIDS, Annie has left Ted's house and wants to get to her car but is confronted by a tall, locked gate.

In the series CHERNOBYL, government officials need to get an accurate measurement of the radiation at the damaged plant but the radiation is too strong to even enter the site.

Things in Absentia

In addition to Things that physically stand in a character's way—rivers, doors, zombies—is a class of Things created by their absence.

Our hypothetical Detective Shovel, for example, may not know exactly what clue he'll find at the crime scene, but he is hoping to discover something specific that will lead to the criminal. The obstacle in this instance is the *absence* of that clue, or his imperfect knowledge of the situation. Of course that absence could be the result of a very careful criminal who hid their tracks earlier when they committed the crime, or it could be because something like time or weather has corrupted the evidence. Either way, poor Detective Shovel can't find what he wants in this scene because it's hidden from him. The absent Thing is a staple obstacle in mysteries.

The obstacle in absentia crops up in survival stories too, where characters are always in need of food and shelter. Some good examples of these appear in THE MARTIAN, INTO THE WILD, CASTAWAY, and THE ROAD.

It's Not You, It's Me

Our third class of obstacles is internal. A character's phobia, self-doubt, self-critique, or personality flaws all fit into this category. Films like THE KING'S SPEECH and FINDING NEMO feature characters who have to overcome something within themselves in order to achieve their goals: King George VI has a stammer, and Marlin's afraid of losing his only child. But what do you actually show on screen when an obstacle is internal?

It's easy: create an external manifestation of the internal obstacle. Suppose your character has a fear of heights. Even though that's purely internal, all you have to do is bring them to the top of a bottomless chasm. By doing so, you pit the character against an external Thing (in this case) or Other that represents the internal obstacle. Indiana Jones is terrified of snakes, so of course the writers are going to toss him into a pit with hundreds of them.

> In SEX EDUCATION (Season 1, Episode 6), Otis wants to lose his virginity with his schoolmate Lily, but his complex relationship with his own sexuality gets in the way.

> In a middle school pool party scene from EIGHTH GRADE, Kayla has to face her fears of being an unwanted outsider among the clique of popular kids.

> In a scene from WHEN HARRY MET SALLY, Harry's commitment phobia comes to a head when he wakes up next to Sally after their first night together.

EXERCISE: Exploring the Possibilities

For each of the categories above (Other, Thing, and Self), dream up two or three new obstacles to impede your character from reaching their scene goal. Even though some might not make sense given how you were imagining your story (such as killer robots in a romantic comedy), have fun surveying the range of options. Identifying what your obstacle is NOT can help you zero in on what it absolutely must be.

Remember: in a Character versus Other situation, you need to give the Other a clear and mutually exclusive goal of their own.

Try following this model:

CHARACTER cannot SCENE GOAL because OBSTACLE.

Here are some (often silly) examples from our developing stories:

OTHER: Betty cannot get her purse back because the bouncer won't let her in.

THING: Betty cannot get her purse back because the dance club is on fire.

SELF: Betty cannot get her purse back because the DJ is playing Europop and she cannot abide Europop.

And:

OTHER: Kara cannot dance with Janelle because Janelle doesn't want to dance with her.

THING: Kara cannot dance with Janelle because the dance floor is too crowded.

SELF: Kara cannot dance with Janelle because she's too shy to even approach her.

And:

OTHER: Detective Shovel cannot find the clue because the criminal was too clever in concealing his steps.

THING: Detective Shovel cannot find the clue because the victim's guard dog won't let him in the house.

SELF: Detective Shovel cannot find the clue because he's nauseated by the smell of mothballs permeating the site.

The Just Right Obstacle

Brainstorming is fun and all, but what from the infinite universe of obstacles is the perfect thing to throw in your character's way, and how will you know when you've found it?

The ideal obstacle will resonate with your script's world, tone, and theme.

We consider these categories in detail below, but as an overall guideline: Trust your instincts. Even though your scene is unwritten, it already exists in your imagination in some form. If an obstacle feels off to you, it probably is, even if you can't clearly articulate why (yet).

Also, as you will see, your choice of obstacle will help *define* your script's world, tone, and theme. So if that choice begins taking your story in a direction that isn't what you want, throw it out and consider other options.

As you embark on the quest for the perfect obstacle, remember that you're trying to make your scene into a great bout. An event for the ages. So you need to choose an obstacle that is a perfect fit for your character at this point in their journey. An encounter that will test and shape them for the rest of their lives.

Resonance with World and Tone

When we refer to your story's *world*, we're talking about all the kinds of things that are possible (or not) in your story's unique universe. Is it medieval or post-apocalyptic? Is it a techno-centric future or an antiquated past? Is it like our world today, or radically different? Socio-politically, is it stable or tumbling into anarchy? Is it an oligarchy or a democracy or something else entirely? What are the rules? Do animals talk? Do people fly?

> In SCOTT PILGRIM VS. THE WORLD, vegans have special powers and Scott must battle with Ramona's angry exes in order to be her boyfriend.

In THE LORD OF THE RINGS, the characters encounter magical rings and anthropomorphic talking trees.

In the world of PRINCESS MONONOKE, an iron bullet can poison a giant animal spirit and curse a human boy, and hunters can cut off the head of a god.

In WESTWORLD, near-human robots in a theme park for the ultra-rich stage a revolution after developing self-awareness.

Be warned: the obstacles you choose must remain consistent with the qualities of your world. In other words, if you're telling a real-world story, you will be limited to real-world obstacles. If you're going to create something more fantastical, you'll still need to adhere to an internal logic that you devise in order to manage your readers' expectations. For example, if you establish that laser beams kill people, a lot of readers will tune out if you suddenly have someone survive a laser blast without explanation.

Tone is a somewhat squishier term that we use to stand for the overall feeling you're trying to create with your story (and therefore your scene). For example, a scene's tone might be dark or light, serious or funny, brooding or playful, sad or happy, cute or horrific, serious or absurd, and so on.

The tone of HEATHERS is hilarious and disturbing.

NO COUNTRY FOR OLD MEN is brooding and terrifying.

BOOKSMART is funny and poignant.

Tone is important because serious scenes demand serious obstacles. It wouldn't make sense for a warrior in an action thriller to be sidelined by a bee sting. And the same applies for light-hearted scenes: a kid trying to get to school on time in an all-ages comedy probably won't be kidnapped by ruthless gang members.

Let's look closer at Betty's situation within the context of world and tone. As a reminder, she wants to get back into that exclusive nightclub to recover her purse.

Assume for a moment that Betty's story is a serious, realistic, contemporary drama. If that's the case, then her scene obstacle is probably not a fire-breathing dragon. It's also probably not likely to be a flood, a high-tech voice-activated steel door, or a misogynistic military presence that forbids women in bars. As we filter through these Character versus Thing scenarios that don't fit, we're left with simple Things like a nightclub that is closed and locked up for the night with Betty's purse still inside.

What about Self and Other as possible obstacles? The whole class of Character versus Self obstacles doesn't really jibe with this story's realistic tone since Betty was already inside the club. Any fear of crowds she might have, or distaste for loud music, would have already been triggered from her earlier visit. Unless she has some strange phobia of admitting her own mistakes to strangers, we can probably rule out the Character versus Self category entirely.

In narrowing our choices through this world and tone filter, it becomes more and more likely that her scene obstacle would be an Other. One obvious choice would be the club's bouncer or security guard. This may not be the most creative antagonist, but it passes our quick world and tone check.

Now take Kara, the seventh grader at the junior high formal, who desperately wants to dance with her crush Janelle. What is keeping her from achieving her scene goal?

Let's imagine that this scene is from a present-day coming-of-age comedy. Given this setting, Kara's obstacle isn't a monster or a robot. It may be that another person is literally blocking her way, which could play well in the world of comedy, but it seems a whole lot more likely that Kara's own doubts or fears may be obstructing her goal, which immediately resonates with the coming-of-age awkwardness of middle school. So this could very well be a Character versus Self situation.

If you don't yet know the world and tone of your story, don't worry: you've already started to figure them out by completing the previous exercises and you will continue to refine them as you pin down the obstacle(s) in the next exercise.

Resonance with Theme

Over the course of your story, your characters will be tested by obstacles. Through their successes and failures, you will introduce thematic content. If, for example, a character is rewarded for their stubbornness, it offers a positive theme about determination. As a writer, what character qualities would you like to reward and/or punish? Traits like hubris, virtue, craftiness, loyalty, ignorance, greed, and jealousy can be assets or liabilities, depending on you and your scene.

Let's consider the bouncer standing between Betty and her goal. Why won't he let her back inside the club to get her purse?

Let's say he's a letter-of-the-law kind of guy who simply won't let her in without an ID. Period. It doesn't matter to him that her ID is in her purse, stuck in the nightclub. He's a rule-follower, confident and secure in his job because he knows he is trusted and reliable.

Or perhaps he doesn't believe her story about the purse. He doesn't remember her entering the nightclub earlier, so he thinks she's just cooking up an excuse to skip the long line.

Maybe he's caught up in his own little power trip as the guy in charge. He's a petty tyrant out to make others feel small.

Note that all three of these were chosen with the previously assumed world and tone in mind. Had we been in a different universe, or telling a story with a different feeling, we would have come up with different bouncers.

No matter what motives we choose for the bouncer's opposition, we are going to want some fundamental contrast between his beliefs and Betty's. For example, if Betty is a rule-breaker, then the letter-of-the-law kind of bouncer provides a great contrast. If she's earnest, the bouncer could suspect her of lying. If she's kind, considerate, and polite, perhaps he can be a manipulative and misogynistic jerk.

In other words, the obstacle isn't just some random obstruction. Make it a foil to your character's value system. Tailor the obstacle to fit the object lesson(s) you want your character and reader to learn. This approach will make the conflict ideological, and the encounter in turn will be an object lesson where two value systems clash head to head.

Let's take a look at some example scenes and how their obstacles resonate with the worlds, tones, and themes of their larger stories.

The world of GET OUT looks like contemporary New York and its bucolic surroundings, but quickly proves to be a sci-fi future in which minds can be transferred between bodies. It is disarmingly scary in tone. The story teaches that the progressive "post-racial" paradise America pretends it has become is a big lie told by white people so that they can continue to exploit black bodies for their own benefit.

In one scene, Chris just wants to go back to bed after having a late-night smoke. He's hypnotized, however, by Missy, whose powers remain consistent with the world of the story. Chris's terrifying psychological journey through hypnosis is tonally spot-on, and Missy's entitled invasion of his most private memories is fully resonant with the film's larger theme. She is the perfect obstacle at that moment.

EIGHTH GRADE centers on a contemporary middle school in the United States. Tonally, it approaches a documentary realism, sitting patiently with Kayla's moments of pleasure and discomfort alike. Thematically, the film suggests that fighting to be someone you're not is much harder and ultimately less rewarding than accepting who you really are.

In one scene, Kayla is at the dinner table with her father on a Friday night. She wants to keep scrolling through her iPhone but Dad wants to talk. He tells her she's great and encourages her to put herself out there more so her peers will see it, implying she should go to fellow eighth grader Kennedy's upcoming pool party. As an obstacle, Dad pits Kayla's easy, familiar, escapist iPhone world (chock-full of carefully cultivated faux identities) directly against the painful reality of the real world that Kayla wants to be a part of but hasn't figured out yet. His voice echoes her own, recalling sentiments that she knows are true but that she struggles to embody.

The world of MONTY PYTHON AND THE HOLY GRAIL is a medieval Arthurian legend that rises to absurdist heights when anachronistic British police officers show up to arrest the Knights of the Round Table. Thematically, the film encourages its audiences to question authoritative and pristine versions of history by presenting our legendary heroes behaving in less-than-heroic ways.

In one scene, King Arthur simply wants to find out from a peasant who lives in a particular castle. The peasant doesn't tell him, challenging the authority and power that Arthur (as King) takes for granted. The peasant is a perfect obstacle for Arthur's entitlement. To the peasant, Arthur's just a bossy guy making too many assumptions.

EXERCISE: What Story Does This Obstacle Tell?

The previous exercise gave you a list of obstacles to consider. Start by ruling out any that you know aren't working, and then winnow down the rest until you're left with two or three. If you don't have that many, take a minute to explore some new options. As a reminder, try to articulate them using the following model:

CHARACTER cannot SCENE GOAL because OBSTACLE.

You know a lot about your story; for now, pretend that you're a reader experiencing your scene for the first time. From this perspective, answer the following questions about each of the obstacles you're considering:

1   What can you ascertain or assume about the world of this story, given this goal and obstacle? Is it modern-day, past, or present? What kind of rules are in place? What is the governing body like? Is it like our world or entirely different?

2   What can you ascertain or assume about the tone of this story, given the goal and obstacle you've selected? Is it wacky, dark, serious, hilarious, realistic, over-the-top, terrifying?

3 What lessons or themes might emerge simply from seeing this character face this obstacle? Does this match-up pit ignorance against experience? Independence against authority? Selfishness against selflessness?

The obstacles that are the best candidates for your scene are those that are most expressive of, and resonant with, the world, tone, and/or theme that you want your story to embody.

Time Isn't on Your Side

No matter what type of obstacle your character is facing, you can make it more of a challenge if you limit the resources they have available.

Take time, for instance.

Betty wants her purse back. Let's assume a bouncer is standing in her way. If she has time to flirt with the bouncer, ask him on a date, spend years getting to know him and then sneak out one night past their four sleeping children to recover the purse, your story has gone well off the rails.

But if time is limited, things get much more interesting. Perhaps the club is closing so the bouncer can't stand around arguing. Or maybe Betty has to catch a bus. Both options create what is known as a *ticking clock* that amplifies the obstacle.

Note that you can limit the other resources your character has available, too. Suppose you have a character who needs to cross a raging river. That obstacle doesn't look so bad if your character has a raft, but what if all they have is a spoon?

Be sure that any limitations emerge naturally and logically from the story you're telling; otherwise your readers will see right through the false constraint. For example, imagine that Detective Shovel can't look for clues because a radiator breaks and fills the crime scene with steam. Feels a little random, doesn't it? There must be a logical reason for that break if the story is to remain grounded in realism. Maybe Shovel kicked it in frustration, making the impediment emerge directly from an aspect of his character.

Here are a few additional examples:

> Molly and Amy don't have a lot of time to debate going to a high school party in BOOKSMART because it's literally their last night of high school.

> It gets even harder to make it to the pageant in LITTLE MISS SUNSHINE when the family van has a bad clutch and a horn that attracts the attention of cops.

> Getting away from thieves who want to kill you is pretty intense, but to have to run over a floor covered in shattered glass with bare feet makes John McClane's challenge even harder in a scene from DIE HARD.

EXERCISE: Limit the Resources, and Pick

For any obstacle(s) you still have in mind, list two or three ways you could limit your character's resources to enhance the obstacle's difficulty. Time is an obvious choice, but don't forget that you can take away money, shoes, oxygen, and really anything you can think of in order to make their situation stickier.

After that, it's time to choose. Circle the best obstacle you have to take with you into the next phase of planning. And if it isn't yet perfect, there will be plenty of opportunities to revise later, if and when you come up with something better.

3 What Are They Gonna Do about It?

Betty wants her purse back but the bouncer won't let her back into the club. Kara wants to ask Janelle to dance but she's immobilized by shyness. Detective Shovel wants to find a clue but the criminal left a pristine crime scene. What are they all to do?

Easy: they're going to *act*. As these setups all suggest, when you obstruct a character in pursuit of a goal, they're gonna do something about it. Your character won't take the obstacle lying down. They'll try to navigate around whatever's in their way.

Don't Just Stand There, Do Something!

How your character acts to confront an obstacle (what we call their *approach*) is where your character's *character* emerges for the reader. This is why we put obstacles in the way of our characters: so that our readers can see who they truly are.

A character's actions in the face of adversity will showcase their values, their priorities, and their worldview. Their actions will also allow readers to see when a character is confused, mistaken, ignorant, clever, or bold. Picture that poor guy leaning in to push the door marked "pull" for the umpteenth time. He's certainly dedicated, probably stubborn, and isn't gonna get anywhere until he figures out that he's going about it in entirely the wrong way.

Or take Hamlet, for example. Here is someone who feigns his own madness so that he can investigate his father's murder without suspicion. If he was never confronted with anything more challenging than peeling a pile of potatoes, the complexity of his character would remain buried.

New writers sometimes think that "developing characters" means laying out a bunch of backstory, things like where the characters grew up or the circumstances of their lives before your story begins. But true *character development* for readers occurs when they see characters acting in the present. So save your characters' backstories for your own research, and focus on showing them getting things done now.

You Talkin' to Me? (Characters versus Others)

When a character faces an Other, you've got two sentient folks with different goals who are each trying to get what they want.

We all have a lot of experience being in this situation, going way back to when we were hungry babies desperate to get our caregivers to stop whatever they were doing and feed us. And unless you live like a hermit today, you still have these kinds of encounters all the time: you want your toddler to go to bed but they want to stay up; you want chicken for dinner but everyone else wants pasta; you want the trash company to reimburse you but they insist you were the one that accidently dropped that garbage can through your car window.

What's a character to do? Well, here are some of the many, many ways characters might go about getting what they want:

Barter	Embarrass	Lecture
Blackmail	Empathize	Seduce
Bribe	Entertain	Shame
Bully	Extort	Silence
Cajole	Flatter	Sympathize
Charm	Humor	Tell the truth
Debate	Interrogate	Threaten
Deceive	Intimidate	

Returning to the examples we introduced in the last chapter of characters facing Others:

Anna wants to play with Maya's brother in PEN15 but Maya wants them to play on their own. They launch into a debate about the rules of common courtesy. Anna argues that her status as guest means she should get to choose. Maya claims the privilege of host. Anna reminds Maya that they consider each other sisters, which means that she too should have host privileges. Beaten in this debate of middle school logic, Maya finally concedes.

The Dread Pirate Roberts deceives The Sicilian in THE PRINCESS BRIDE. He presents two goblets to his brilliant and devious opponent, suggesting that one is poisoned and one is not. All The Sicilian must do is pick one and Roberts will drink from the other. But the truth is that both goblets are poisoned and Roberts has spent years developing an immunity.

To get the reluctant witness to talk in the pilot of THE WIRE, McNulty ultimately bribes him with three Newports and a grape Nehi. It's a moment we don't see on-screen, but we hear about later in the episode when McNulty recounts the story to a colleague.

Sometimes conflict can turn violent. But even if your characters are throwing punches instead of insults, they're still making choices that define who they are, what they value, and what they still have to learn. So choose their actions as carefully in a physical conflict as you'd choose the words for a verbal one.

Consider Gandalf versus the Balrog in THE LORD OF THE RINGS: THE FELLOWSHIP OF THE RING. To protect the rest of the Fellowship, he faces the huge demonic beast alone, delivering the memorable line, "You shall not pass!" It's an act of selfless bravery writ large.

In a similar situation (with a radically different tone) from MONTY PYTHON AND THE HOLY GRAIL, Arthur faces the Black Knight, who will not let him cross a bridge. Arthur tries to get him to move with words, but the Black Knight won't have it. At last swords are drawn. Arthur outmatches the knight and severs one of his arms. The battle should be over. But no! The knight absurdly presses on. Arthur severs another limb, only to be egged on further. Only after Arthur completely dismembers the knight can he cross the bridge, kindly calling the battle a draw so as to protect the Black Knight's overblown pride.

In SELMA, the first march across the Edmund Pettus Bridge is met with unprovoked violence by state troopers. The march leaders Hosea Williams, John Lewis, and Amelia Boynton, among others, ask for a peaceable word of discussion but learn no considerations will be made. They are told to disperse but stand their ground even as the troopers don gas masks and raise their batons. The marchers sacrifice their bodies, demonstrating to the world the inhumanity of their oppressors.

You Can't Argue with a River (Characters versus Things)

Characters have basically two choices when it comes to navigating the obstacles that are Things. They can either make their way through/across/past the Thing or find an alternative way around. If the obstacle is a locked door, your character can pick the lock, bash the door down, pull it off its hinges, or, if none of those approaches are possible, look for a window. How they proceed, once again, reveals character.

Returning to the examples we introduced in the last chapter:

To get past the countless robots standing between him and Zurg's fortress in TOY STORY 2, Buzz Lightyear shoots his own laser into a nearby crystal, causing the beam to split and multiply and take out the entire army of robots at once. His response is a testament to his quickness of mind and his craftiness.

Annie chooses to scale the tall, locked gate that's keeping her from leaving Ted's house in BRIDESMAIDS because she's too embarrassed and too proud to go back in and ask the guy who just dumped her to open the gate.

To get an accurate measurement of the radiation at the damaged nuclear plant in CHERNOBYL, General Pikalov risks his life to drive a high-range dosimeter directly into the plant to gather the data they need. He is brave and willing to do anything to help his country circumvent this disaster.

I'm My Own Worst Enemy (Character versus Self)

When your character's biggest scene obstacle is themselves, then they have to get out of their own way. Sounds tricky, right? Well, as mentioned in the last chapter, even deep-seated internal obstacles will be expressed in terms of an external obstacle, creating a more traditional Character versus Other or Character versus Thing conflict. Any difference will lie in the limit of choices available to your character.

Let's say someone has spent the better part of a movie chasing after what Alfred Hitchcock referred to as the *MacGuffin*—a Thing like a rare diamond, a love letter, the buried treasure, you know the deal. In your scene they finally have the chance to grab what they want, but they are deathly afraid of spiders, and there's an itty-bitty one sitting on top of it.

For most people, this is no obstacle. They flick the spider away, grab the MacGuffin, and ride off into the sunset. But because of their phobia, your character is bound by limited options. What are easy or rational choices to most people simply aren't available to them. This internal obstacle must be set up in advance so it doesn't appear out of nowhere in the scene. But if foreshadowed properly, the audience will understand the truth of your character's internal obstacle and relate to their struggle to navigate it, even if they don't share that exact fear.

In the aforementioned scene from SEX EDUCATION (Season 1, Episode 6), Otis wants to lose his virginity with his schoolmate Lily. He finally has his chance, she's willing, he's willing, they're alone in a safe place. It should be a done deal. But the intimacy brings back unhappy memories of his father's infidelity, triggering a panic attack.

An end-of-semester pool party should be fun for everyone, but it's torture for shy Kayla in EIGHTH GRADE. Though she wants to be like everyone else, Kayla has to psych herself up just to get out of the bathroom. She squeezes her way through a jammed door and past dozens of other frolicking kids. When she finally reaches the pool, all she can manage is to hide herself deep in the water.

In WHEN HARRY MET SALLY, the two main characters finally sleep together following years of on-and-off friendship. For anyone else, the next morning would be a happily-ever-after moment. But Harry's commitment issues cause him to self-sabotage it instead.

Getting By with a Little Help from My Friends

No matter what kind of obstacle they're up against in your scene—Other, Thing, or Self—your characters could probably use a helping hand. It's the rare movie like CASTAWAY that features a truly solo protagonist receiving zero assistance. Even Mark Watney, stranded alone on Mars in THE MARTIAN, is aided by his NASA friends on Earth.

Allies can help in all sorts of ways. They can point out flaws in your main character's plan, saving them from failure, or suggest an entirely new strategy that may work better. They might also just serve as an extra hand, or leg, or back that your main character needs to intimidate the opponents or smash down a door.

Be aware that allies shouldn't solve the entire problem for your character. In extreme cases, referred to as *deus ex machina*, someone or something appears out of nowhere to help your character escape a seemingly inescapable bind. When this happens, you lose all the drama (and enjoyment) that comes from watching the main character struggle for what they want.

By contrast, it can be exhilarating when an ally helps your main character overcome an obstacle, *if that help is the result of something your main character did earlier*. In other words, when the ally's decisions were set up by earlier interactions and struggles, and then they swoop in to assist your main character, it can result in an unexpected yet satisfying resolution. In that case it's not deux ex machina, it's fruit grown from seeds that were planted earlier.

> In STAR WARS, as Luke zooms in for a final attack on the Death Star, Han Solo returns out of nowhere to knock Darth Vader off of Luke's tail. But it's not really out of nowhere, because throughout the film Luke has directly and repeatedly challenged Han's selfishness. It becomes clear at this moment that Han was actually listening and has changed for the better.

> In DIE HARD, hero John McClane is about to be killed by a terrorist, but he's saved at the last minute when officer Al shoots the terrorist dead. Of course Al was only able to pull the trigger because McClane had earlier consoled him about the accident that had been haunting Al.

> In CHERNOBYL, Professor Legasov is unable to complete his important and damning testimony because the powers-that-be choose to end the trial early. But the more powerful Shcherbina demands that they let him finish, an action that wouldn't have happened had he and Legasov not scrapped earlier about the value of truth versus the preservation of the state.

EXERCISE: Exploring Approaches

Set a timer for ten minutes and brainstorm specific approaches your character could attempt to get around the obstacle confronting them. Keep your pen moving (or fingers typing)—there are no bad ideas here.

Try using the following model to help you articulate why your character chooses their particular approach:

CHARACTER tries APPROACH because REASON.

The approach and the reason for it reflect your character's values and priorities at the time, as well as their (possibly flawed) understanding of the situation facing them.

Here are some examples from our developing stories:

In the case of Betty and the bouncer:

Betty tries flirting with the bouncer because she thinks she can manipulate him.

Betty tries threatening to call the manager on the bouncer because she thinks he will cave to a threat.

Betty tries knocking out the bouncer because she thinks she's in the right, she can take him, and she can't abide his utter lameness.

In the case of Kara being too shy to approach Janelle:

Kara tries asking Janelle to dance because she no longer cares about the consequences.

Kara tries catching Janelle's eye with some amazing dance moves she's been practicing for this very purpose because anyone in their right mind would find them awesome like she does.

Kara tries slipping a note into Janelle's pocket because she believes she'll screw it up if she tries asking in person.

In the case of Detective Shovel and the sophisticated criminal:

Detective Shovel tries recreating the crime in his head yet again because he's convinced that no one's perfect, not even this criminal, and that there must be a clue if only he could see it.

Detective Shovel tries bringing in the young star detective of the department because he worries that he's slipping and might miss something.

Detective Shovel tries setting off a bug bomb, potentially destroying the crime scene, because he believes the chemical reactions will reveal a hidden clue.

It's Only a Mistake if You Don't Learn From It

Your character wants something but there's an obstacle in the way so they devise an approach to get what they want and they act upon it.

Whether or not your character gets what they want in the end (we come to that in the next section), it's worth taking a close look at the high value of failure. Failed attempts are wonderful teachers. When a character fails, it gives them the opportunity to learn about themselves and the world they inhabit. This opportunity, in turn, allows them to adjust their approach to navigating the obstacles they face.

> Betty attempts to flirt with the bouncer ... but then he mentions his husband. Maybe sincerity would work instead?
>
> Kara tries to impress Janelle with some dance moves ... but she accidentally kicks the principal. Maybe she should try a more straightforward approach?
>
> Detective Shovel attempts to dust for prints ... but oddly there isn't a single print to be found. Maybe he can subpoena the neighbors' security cameras?

When you make your character fail, you're breaking them out of their complacency, their ingrained habits, and their assumptions. Failure snaps your character to attention, telling them, "you don't know everything!" It makes them think on their feet and improvise a new approach to getting what they want. Will your character give up and find a new goal? Will they try something clever or violent or hilarious? Will they succumb to their emotions or face the obstacle with an icy determination? The answers will reveal their character.

Given the value of failure, consider having your character take multiple unsuccessful strikes at an obstacle. Each one will provide a new opportunity to see them adapt. There's no rule for how many, but three is a good place to begin. Goldilocks examines three beds, and by trying each of them out, she learns that one is too soft, one is too hard, and one is just right.

Like Goldilocks, with each failed attempt your character will hopefully discover something new about the world and/or themselves, information they can use as their journey continues. For example, next time, instead of obsessing over the furniture, maybe Goldilocks will look for signs of bears.

Themes Like a Good Idea

Let's say that your character tries to achieve their scene goal through bribery. But it fails. Do they pivot, and ask nicely instead? Break down in tears? Or do they throw even more money down on the table? By rewarding one of these approaches over the other, you provide a thematic object lesson to your reader.

The following scenes feature characters who try multiple times to get what they want. Some learn from their failures, some don't (which also says something important about their character). Thematic content emerges from each scene, in either case:

In QUEEN & SLIM, the titular protagonists are pulled over by Officer Reed. Fearing for his life, Slim does everything he can to comply with Reed's orders, but to no avail. The officer continues to harass Slim until Queen loses patience and Reed recklessly draws his gun and fires. Slim leaps to Queen's defense, wrestles the gun from the officer and shoots him dead. Slim gets out of the encounter alive, as he hoped, but at an enormous cost. Thematically, it's clear that all of Slim's attempts to appease the racist cop were in vain; the outcome was written in blood from the start.

In THE INCREDIBLES, Bob's (aka Mr. Incredible's) overconfidence in his own abilities causes him to underestimate the deadly Omnidroid when he first encounters it. Unbeknownst to Bob, the robot learns as they fight, so it pretty quickly outclasses his out-of-shape older self. The new robot looks like it's going to take down Bob with ease... until Bob craftily figures out that he can get the robot to focus all of its destructive power on itself. He wins because he out-thinks rather than out-muscles the thing.

In DIE HARD, John McClane wants the police to come to Nakatomi Plaza, where terrorists are holding hostages. The 911 operators think McClane is pranking them, but they send over officer Al just in case. McClane believes he's succeeded in getting assistance but the terrorists have outsmarted him, making everything appear normal to Al from the outside. As he turns to leave, McClane realizes he's failed. With a bit of quick thinking, he throws a dead terrorist out the window. The body smashes into Al's car, obviously getting his attention. Success! The action demonstrates McClane's ingenuity and headstrong personality—traits that ultimately save both the hostages and his marriage.

EXERCISE: So THAT Didn't Work . . .

In this exercise, you'll take each of your brainstormed approaches from the last exercise and make them all fail. As you do, highlight what your character learns that will help them out next time, and also what thematic lesson emerges from the failure.

Feel free to brainstorm more wonderful failures too!

Try the following model:

CHARACTER tries APPROACH because REASON. But they fail because of DISCOVERY.

LESSON: After each failure, add a thematic lesson that the character should learn from the experience.

Here are some examples from our developing stories:

Betty tries flirting with the bouncer because she thinks she can manipulate him. But she has to pivot her strategy when he mentions his husband.

LESSON: Betty should realize that maybe sincerity is a better avenue than manipulation.

Kara tries slipping a note into Janelle's pocket because she's scared of being rejected face-to-face. But the attempt doesn't work because Janelle never reaches into her pocket.

LESSON: Kara shouldn't be so afraid of failure that she never tries anything.

Detective Shovel tries bringing in the young star detective of the department because he worries that he's slipping and might miss something. But the new guy rushes through and ruins a piece of evidence.

LESSON: Shovel should trust more in his decades of experience.

Where're You Going with This?

Setting up a scene around a goal provides two possible *resolutions* for the scene: your character either gets what they want or they don't.

Which should you choose?

The answer will shape everything that happens next in your story. Will this be a dramatic uptick or a downturn in your character's journey? Will they make progress towards their overarching goal or be stymied and have to try something different?

Suppose your character overcomes the obstacle and achieves their scene goal: Betty successfully flirts her way around the bouncer and back into the club. We call this an *up ending*. Now, let's hope her purse is still there.

By contrast, if your main character doesn't get what they want, then they're going to have to attempt a new way around the obstacle or abandon what they were after: Betty tries but simply can't convince the bouncer to let her skip the line. This is a *down ending*. What's she going to do now?

Bear in mind that it's rarely the case that an *up ending* is purely up and that a *down ending* is purely down. The successful attainment of a scene goal will likely come at a cost, either literal or emotional. And failure—as we explored earlier—often comes with a realization, a lesson, or a discovery that will ultimately help your character further down the line.

> In BOOKSMART, Molly and Amy want to get to a party but they don't know the address. What they do know is that Lido's Pizza delivered a huge order to the same party earlier that night. So they pretend to stick up a Lido's delivery guy and scare the information out of him. Their terrible plan doesn't work out as expected, but amazingly, they get the address they need. This up ending for the scene propels them one step closer to their overarching goal of getting to the party, but at the cost of a pretty scary reckoning with their own naiveté and vulnerability.

In LITTLE MISS SUNSHINE, Richard wants to get to Boca Raton for Olive's beauty competition but he cannot abandon the dead body of his father-in-law at the hospital, nor can he take it across state lines without a permit. With the help of his family, they sneak the body out a window and into their van. This up ending sees them successfully back on the road, but at the cost of breaking the law.

In GET OUT, Chris very much wants to leave the Armitage family home. He asks Rose for the car keys . . . and she refuses. The scene ends with a down ending, but Chris learns the important (and terrifying) information that Rose is out to kidnap him, too.

In CASABLANCA, Rick wants Ilsa to accept his apology for his angry, bitter behavior when they fought the night before. Despite three different attempts, she refuses. In this down ending, Rick does not attain his scene goal. But he does learn that if he wants to win Ilsa back, he is going to have to let go of his anger.

EXERCISE: So How Does Your Scene End?

If your scene is part of a larger story that you've mapped out, you already know if your character will get their scene goal or not. But if you're writing something new, you might not be sure. In that case, do this exercise twice, once where your character succeeds and once where they fail.

If your character succeeds (up ending), brainstorm five different costs for that success. What might they have to sacrifice, endure, or lose in order to get what they wanted? This could be a physical thing (like money, a broken arm, tickets to the Mets game), or something less tangible but still real for them (like time, embarrassment, angering a friend, breaking a promise to themselves or another).

If they fail (down ending), you've already got a head start on the many things they might learn from their failure. But try to come up with five more. What might they gain, realize, and/or understand that could help them later on?

Try matching the following models:

> Success: CHARACTER gets SCENE GOAL, but at a COST.
>
> Failure: CHARACTER doesn't get SCENE GOAL, but gains a REWARD.

Here are some examples from our developing stories:

> Betty gets her purse back, but now she has to go out on a date with the creepy bouncer.
>
> Betty doesn't get her purse back, but she felt good when everyone in line started chanting to let her back inside.
>
> Kara gets Janelle to dance with her, but not before embarrassing herself in front of the whole school.
>
> Kara doesn't get to dance with Janelle, but she does get her phone number.
>
> Detective Shovel finds an errant hair at the crime scene, but he ticked off his partner in the process.
>
> Detective Shovel doesn't find a specific clue at the crime scene, but he realizes that might be a clue in and of itself, so he begins looking for a criminal who has OCD.

Not All Actions Are Created Equal

At this stage you've generated a lot of options for what your character might do in order to get what they want. To select and order the best approaches for your scene, consider the idea of *stakes* and also how those attempts fit into your story's world and tone.

Cooking Up Stakes

All the actions that we take come with costs and risks. If you want to climb a mountain peak, your costs might include the gas to get there, the time and energy it takes you to hike up, and so forth. The risks include falling from the top, twisting your ankle, frostbite, dehydration, and the like. And yet you do it anyway despite these *stakes*, because the benefits of climbing that peak are worth it. It's exhilarating.

When people act, they do so because they believe the rewards of their actions outweigh the stakes. It's the same with your characters. What is on the line as they navigate their obstacle? What are they willing to risk in order to attain their goal?

It makes sense for your characters to attempt the lowest stakes option first. Why bribe the maître d' for a prime table with a thousand bucks when a twenty might work? Of course, if the maître d' laughs at the twenty, your character can move to a higher-stakes option or find a new restaurant.

Having your characters work from low to higher stakes will inform your reader about your character's values. Some characters, after all, might open with a thousand and think nothing of it. Others might balk at any suggestion of bribery.

Note that we're not raising the stakes by changing the obstacle. In JAWS, raising the stakes doesn't mean adding more sharks. For the character Brody, the stakes go up as he gets closer and closer to being eaten by the beast after each failed attempt to kill it.

Consider Kara wanting to dance with Janelle. We all know the kind of people who—even in middle school—could waltz up to their crush, ask them to dance, and not really care if they said yes or no. If Kara's that kind of kid, this is a low-stakes situation and might not create a very exciting scene. Much more interesting is the version of Kara who's terrified of humiliation, rejection, and embarrassment, but still willing to risk it.

Earlier we came up with three approaches for how Kara might approach Janelle. How do they measure up in terms of stakes for this shyer and more nervous version of Kara?

By slipping a note into Janelle's pocket, Kara avoids face-to-face humiliation at the dance. A good low stakes option. If she hops on the dance floor to show off her killer moves, she will call a lot of attention to herself, but then again, she's not directly at risk of rejection by Janelle. So those stakes are slightly higher. If, however, Kara crosses the crowded gymnasium and outright asks Janelle to dance, well, that puts everything on the line ranging from private embarrassment to public humiliation. Pretty high stakes for a shy kid like Kara.

Let's consider the stakes at play in a few examples from other scripts:

> When Lady Bird jumps out of the car on page 4 of LADY BIRD, it tells us she is more willing to endure physical harm than to continue arguing with her mother. Everyone has been in a maddening conversation before, but who would jump out of a car to avoid it?

> In EIGHTH GRADE, Kayla goes through a complex ritual of showering, drying her hair, and putting on makeup only to climb back into bed in pajamas to post faux "waking up" pictures to her social media account. Audiences understand the relatable desire to fit in, even if they don't go to the same extremes as Kayla.

> When Kevin reluctantly beats up Chiron in MOONLIGHT, we learn that it's more important for him to fit in with his classmates than it is to protect his friend and lover. It's a choice every audience member will understand even if they might not make it themselves.

It Takes Two to Tango

When your character faces an Other, stakes can work in both directions. In other words, the stakes can go up not just for your character but for the Other too.

Let's imagine Betty tries to guilt the bouncer into letting her go inside. She tells him she's going to miss the bus if she doesn't get her purse back, and if she shows up after curfew her mom will kick her out of the house.

This strategy doesn't put a lot on the line for Betty. What it does instead is show the bouncer the painful implications of his choices. Won't he feel bad if he doesn't let her inside? Does he really want to carry that burden?

Many of the Character versus Other strategies from the first section of this chapter (like "bribe," "threaten," and "charm") work this way. So as you track the stakes in your Character versus Other scene, keep in mind that they can—and probably should—go up for both characters involved.

In a scene from BOOKSMART, Molly wants to convince Amy that they should go to Nick's party on their last night of high school. Molly's first approach is to invoke regret: she tells Amy they'll "always be the girls who missed out." It doesn't work. Molly then appeals to their reputation, how everyone needs to know they're fun as well as smart. That, too, fails. Molly finally gets traction by lying (to her best friend!) and saying that Amy's crush Ryan wants her to come to the party.

In a scene from AMERICAN BEAUTY, Lester quits his job. But he wants to get a year's severance out of his boss Brad. So he threatens to share information that would hurt the company. But when threatening the overall business doesn't work, Lester threatens Brad directly with a bogus harassment charge. Lester has already lost the job and doesn't care about his reputation any more. In this scene, he succeeds by raising the stakes for Brad.

In a scene from GET OUT, Rose, driving, runs into a deer with her car. A cop shows up. Rose and Chris just want to put this accident behind them and continue on with their trip, but the cop asks for Chris's ID. Chris complies, but Rose calls out the cop for what she and he both know is racial profiling, raising the stakes for all involved. It's tense for a moment as the cop assesses whether to drop this or not, but ultimately Rose's white privilege pays off and the officer backs down.

Matching World and Tone

Just like your choice of obstacle from the last chapter, what you have your characters do in order to achieve their goals must support the world and tone of the story you're writing.

If your story is rooted in realism, then the approaches need to be realistic. But if your story is goofy and odd, then so should be your characters' actions.

In SCOTT PILGRIM VS. THE WORLD, Scott wants to ask out Ramona Flowers but he doesn't know how to get in touch with her. He does know that she delivers packages, so he orders something from Amazon and sits by the door, waiting for her to show up. Even his roommate Wallace thinks it's an absurd plan, but in the wacky world of the story, it works!

In GET OUT, Chris wants to leave the late-night conversation he's having with Rose's mother, Missy, but he can't because she has hypnotized him so deeply that she has taken away his bodily control. It's a scary, twisted experience that's likely never happened to anyone in the audience except in their nightmares, but in the world of that film, it is a terrific, palpable obstacle.

In a scene from MOONLIGHT, Juan teaches Little how to swim. Totally resonant with the dramatic realism of the film, the scene is a slow process of gaining Little's trust, one step at a time, by physically supporting him the entire way. The victories are at once minor—floating, treading, trying to paddle—and major, because having a responsible adult in his life allows Little a taste of the childhood he has never really had.

EXERCISE: One Full Approach

Now it's time to synthesize a complete plan for how your character will approach the obstacle in your scene. Drawing from the lists you've built in the previous exercises, and adding any new ideas that come to mind, choose how your character will act in order to get what they want. If you are going to have your character try more than one strategy, sequence them to increase the stakes with each attempt (for your character and/or the Other they might face).

Remember, too, that the attempts your characters make must fit within the world and tone of your story. Absurd actions make absurd films. Thrilling actions make thrillers.

Capture as many details as you can about the approach(es) themselves, but don't worry about getting them all perfect. As you progress through the book, you'll have plenty of opportunities to revise. At this stage it's important simply to choose one coherent plan of action for your character ending in either success or failure.

Here are some examples from our developing stories:

Betty wants her purse back. The last bus is leaving soon and she needs to catch it to get home. She tries flirting with the bouncer to avoid a long line back into the club. When he mentions his husband, she changes tactics and offers the truth. He is sympathetic and when his boss looks the other way he sneaks Betty past the velvet rope.

Kara wants to ask Janelle to dance but is held back by shyness. She slips a note into Janelle's pocket, but it remains undiscovered. Kara musters her courage and tries catching Janelle's eye with some dance moves she's been practicing for this very purpose. But dancing fails because the floor is so crowded that she accidentally kicks the principal. Embarrassed by the attention, Kara slinks away to the refreshment table.

Detective Shovel wants to find a clue at the crime scene but it's immaculate. He tries bringing in the young star detective of the department, believing he's outclassed on this one and that solving the crime is more important than his pride. But it doesn't work because the young detective is so arrogant that Shovel chews him out (and Shovel should know better than to think he's ready to have another partner again). As the young star detective storms off the site, he sarcastically wishes Shovel good luck finding this murderer with OCD. Shovel lights up and calls one of his junior detectives, asking for the records of all perps known to have OCD.

4 Where And When Is It Gonna Happen?

There's a time and a place for everything. *Where* and *when* your scene takes place will influence all aspects of your storytelling.

If your scene takes place at a bar, then you've reduced the universe of possibilities to places that sell drinks, in countries and eras where such things occur. But what bar exactly? In which town? During which year? And at what time? During what season? A scene set in Chicago on a summer evening during Prohibition may unfold very differently from a bar in a college town one winter night in 2022. What will your characters see and hear? Who will witness the fight? What kind of law enforcement will be called in? What kind of beer gets tossed?

Because of the work you've done already, your audience will care about your character working to achieve their scene goal. But if the scene unfolds in an ambiguous time and place, then you risk losing your reader. The objects your characters interact with, the things they hear, say, and wear, the actions and reactions of other characters—all of these choices stem largely from your choice of time and place.

However, changing settings does not necessarily mean changing scenes.

New scenes often begin in new settings, but don't mistake correlation with causation. As a reminder from the start of the book, great scenes provide information, resolution, and engagement. They do not have to happen in a single place, nor at a single time, though they often do.

> Consider the wonderful montage from THE NAKED GUN: FROM THE FILES OF POLICE SQUAD that showcases a blooming relationship. The courtship takes place over many locations and times, showing two characters transforming from

strangers into lovers. The scene ends on a gag when it's revealed that all these different activities occurred on their very first date.

In short, your scene will continue until it resolves, even if that resolution happens at a different time or place than where the scene began.

It's about Freakin' Time

The time of day you pick for your scene dictates whether it's light or dark outside, if most people are awake or asleep, or if they're breaking for a meal. The day of the week suggests to the audience if people should be at work, school, home, or enjoying a weekend. The month might signal a particular season or holiday.

At the largest scale, the year or era in which you set your scene dictates whether or not your story has cell phones, dinosaurs, serfs, dodo birds, spaceships, or even spoken language. Do people forage for food or buy it in a market? Is this an era of freedom or one of oppression? Is this a future with advanced technology or is it a wasteland of climate disasters?

> Consider Alfred Hitchcock's NORTH BY NORTHWEST, set in 1959 at the height of the cold war. Microfilm is a thing, phones, trains, and cars are ubiquitous, but commercial air travel is still unusual. All of this serves as a backdrop to Roger Thornhill's efforts to avoid capture by a mysterious organization smuggling state secrets. Time of day further plays a part in the famous crop duster scene, as the bright sunshine of midday leaves Thornhill nowhere to hide. It would be a very different scene at night, or in a season other than late summer when snow or fog could give him cover.

The temporal setting is relevant to every story, but it plays a more foundational role in some:

> ALL THE PRESIDENT'S MEN, about the U.S. Watergate scandal, can only take place in 1972.

> GROUNDHOG DAY has to occur on February 2.

The disaster at the core of the CHERNOBYL television series occurred at 1:23:58am on April 26, 1986.

Summer is the only time Duncan can discover the waterpark and beaches of THE WAY WAY BACK.

EXERCISE: Identify Your Moment in Time

Identify the specific moment in time that your scene takes place with as much information as is necessary for your story. In some cases this may be an exact hour, day, month, and year, as in a series like CHERNOBYL. At a minimum, identify the time of day, season, and year or era.

Now take a few minutes to consider how that choice of time might directly impact the main character in your scene. Brainstorm three ways in which it might help and/or hinder them to exist at that specific time, on that specific day, season, and year.

For example:

> It's the annual fall formal at Kara's middle school, a mid-November evening around 8pm. Everyone's dressed to the nines. But since it's a cold night, Janelle wears a denim jacket over her dress, giving Kara an opportunity to slip a note into her pocket.

Location, Location, Location!

Setting, like time, has relevance to your story on different scales. The country in which your scene is set dictates the language and the laws, the geography, and the climate. The specific town impacts things like the dialect, architecture, and ethnic, racial, and economic demographics. The particular building and room will determine who's around, what people are doing, and how loud it is, and may suggest what preoccupies your characters at any particular moment.

Place and time are generally intertwined. The kitchen in a popular restaurant will feel very different on a Friday night than on a Monday morning. The way teenagers talk in California's San Fernando Valley will, like, fer sure totally sound different in the 1980s than, like, any other time. In December in Utah there may be snow forts, while in Sydney it'll be sandcastles.

Even though some of the aforementioned stories like ALL THE PRESIDENT'S MEN and CHERNOBYL are tightly coupled with a specific place, it is possible for a story to revolve around a precise location with a less-than-precise time, like NATIONAL TREASURE (which involves the U.S. Archives) or THE SHAWSHANK REDEMPTION (which has to occur at Shawshank Prison).

As you consider a location for your scene, ask yourself whether it can serve as more than just a setting in which the scene plays out. Can you tie the location more tightly to your character's quest? Location can serve as an obstacle or an ally, it can offer unusual location-specific navigation strategies, and it can reinforce the world and tone of your story.

Consider the following examples:

> The moving car in LADY BIRD's opening scene makes it particularly hard for Lady Bird to avoid the uncomfortable conversation with her mother. Had the conversation happened in, say, a kitchen, she could have just walked out.

> Similarly, in DIE HARD, John McClane has to get off the roof of the Nakatomi Plaza skyscraper before it explodes. Had he been on the ground floor, it would have been easy. But being way up high forces him to tie a firehose around his body before bravely leaping into the void.

> In the opening scene of the pilot episode of THE WIRE, McNulty questions a witness about a recent murder. This could have been set in a police interrogation room, but setting it at the crime scene itself, with the victim's body being bagged right in front of them, foregrounds for the reader the violent environment that both the cops and the local kids call home throughout the series.

Let's think back to Betty and the bouncer. By design we've placed this scene at a dance club, but what's the club like, and where specifically is it? Let's try to make Betty's challenge as difficult as possible. If she can avoid the bouncer and just slide in a side door then there's no obstacle, so the club needs to be locked up like Fort Knox. Imagine velvet ropes, lots of security, the works. Now that she can't sneak around, she has to meet the bouncer face-to-face.

First instincts would suggest a busy club so it's hard for her to get his attention. It's Saturday night. Peak time. Folks are lined up. Maybe he wears a headset and is having conversations with other bouncers that Betty can't even hear. And to make it worse, she has to wait in line just to try and get a word in with the guy.

Let's return to Kara and Janelle at the dance. What choices can we make about location to heighten Kara's challenge? If Kara fears embarrassment, then will it be better for the dance to be more or less crowded? If there are only ten people in the school then everyone will see Kara talk to Janelle, whereas if there are two thousand students then she's more likely to disappear in the crowd.

What else about the setting could heighten Kara's fears of embarrassment? Are her parents chaperoning? Is it a Halloween dance and she's stuck in a horribly awkward costume? Do they have an awards announcement in the middle of the dance and Kara is brought on stage for winning the dorky chemistry prize?[1]

Consider the impact of setting in the following scenes:

> In THE HANDMAID'S TALE Offred discreetly discusses revolutionary plans with a fellow handmaid while walking outside. The risky nature of such conversation is reinforced by the setting, which is full of armed guards and the hanging bodies of people who defied the regime.
>
> In JAWS, Quint's cabin is the site for a planning meeting to hunt down the shark. The dozens of deadly looking shark skeletons covering the walls serve as a reminder of the dangers they're about to face, and underscore Quint's shark-crazed madness.

---

[1] Please note that we think chemistry prizes are cool.

The birthday party in EIGHTH GRADE throws Kayla into the mix with the popular kids. But her feelings of being an outsider are heightened by setting the scene at a pool where all the other kids play together, scantily clad, confident, and happy.

EXERCISE: Zooming in on the Precise Location

Working your way from the largest scales to the smallest, identify the planet, continent, country, city/town, building and finally room where you see your scene taking place. If your scene is outside, choose a specific spot down to the street corner, empty lot, alley, park bench, or shade tree.

Now that you have both a time and a place for your scene, brainstorm possible revisions to both based on the following questions:

> How can this specific time and/or place directly influence my character's struggle to achieve their scene goal?
>
> Does my setting resonate with my story's world and tone?
>
> How do the laws and social mores of that time and place define or limit my characters?

Research and Destroy

Up to now you've relied on your pre-existing knowledge to construct an imagined vision of the specific time and place for your scene. But where did that knowledge come from?

If the place in question is your childhood home, then you have years of experience informing that vision. This should make you an expert, right? Perhaps. But were you really paying close attention to the architecture, the landscaping, and the socio-economic demographics of your neighbors? Or were you busy chasing squirrels?

Now imagine you're trying to write about a place and time you've never personally experienced. In this case, you're likely triangulating your understanding from stories you've heard, seen, or read. You may be remixing the work of other writers who themselves might have been playing on assumptions and stereotypes and guesses. In short, you probably know a lot less than you might think.

Luckily, there is a way to break that cycle. In order to depict your specific time and place with the authenticity it deserves, you need to do some research. And not stuffy librarian research.[2] We're talking fun research.

Let's return to Betty and the club. Say we've chosen to set that scene in Miami, on a hot July Saturday night in 2015. Depending on the kind of media you consume, and your age, your pre-existing images of Miami might come from MIAMI VICE, BALLERS, MOONLIGHT, SCARFACE, CSI: MIAMI, or all of the above. They might contain neon signs, beaches, a diverse mix of skin tones, fancy cars, drugs, alcohol, extreme wealth, or extreme poverty. And all those images came to you through an interpretive chain of writers, art directors, set designers, directors, actors, cinematographers and more.

It's time to see it with your own eyes. Sure, you could book a ticket to Miami, but we happen to be writing this book in an era where all sorts of information is accessible through a few gestures on a device. And a lot of that information comes in the form of images.

At this stage of planning your scene, you will get great value from just looking at photographs. Think of it as a virtual location scout. The work you've done so far has given you a range of key terms that define the broad strokes of your scene's location, even if you don't realize it yet. For Betty in particular, these are things like dance club, Miami, velvet ropes, bouncer, 2015, and so on.

Barring some surprising seismic shift in how digital information is shared, a quick look into the terms you've identified should yield plenty of image examples. One image generally leads to another, and before long you will have immersed yourself in the visual expression of a specific place and time.

As an example: a whirlwind virtual photo tour of Miami clubs features things like palm trees, fish tanks, linen suits, gold chains, lots of colored lights, people

---

[2] Please also note that we think librarians are cool.

laughing, and plastic surgeons. These new discoveries may not translate directly into actionable items for the scene yet, but it'll be a great start to record them for the next stage of the scenewriting process (Part II: Drafting).

Photos are extremely valuable, but there's much more to a space than just what you see. What does it sound like? Is there music? Street noise? Are there environmental noises like crickets, waves, or rustling leaves? What languages are being spoken? What accents? Video searches can be helpful here, as can a physical visit if budgets and timelines allow.

If you do get to visit, look and listen but also try and notice whether the place has unique smells, tastes, even feelings. Is someone baking bread? Smoking? Washing the sidewalk? You can communicate these features to your audience indirectly by way of what your characters say and how they emote. For example, send a tourist down the stairs into the New York subway on a pungent summer day and they're bound to make a face or say something about the smell, the noise, the heat.

Newspaper and magazine articles make great research sources and are easily accessible too. Because they're written, they can offer you a way to see how other writers establish a time and/or location through words rather than pictures. How do other authors paint the space for their readers, and can you learn from their approaches?

Allow your interests and imagination to wander during the research phase. Your ultimate goal is to render a compelling and representative written version of the time and place you are imagining, but you will need to do so in an efficient way that doesn't detract from the larger story you're telling. The goal of the research phase is therefore to fill your imagination (and notebook) with images and terms and sounds that you can draw from to place the reader right where and when you want them to be.

EXERCISE: Research and Character Preoccupations

Using the location and time you identified in the prior exercises, do some online image searches using at least two different sites/databases/sources. Save the images that speak to you, even if you can't articulate why. Try and build up a small library of reference images.

Look closely at what you've collected. What catches your attention? What elements make this space and time unique, memorable, and authentic? What sounds, smells, or sights are prominent or notable? It might be posters or paintings on the wall, architectural features, the kinds of people there, or what they're doing.

Now select at least three notable things from your research to incorporate into your scene's location, whatever you found that most brings the space to life for you. For example:

Outside the club, a neon green palm tree towers above Betty.

Finally, identify at least three ways that your characters could interact with and be affected by the location. Specifically, what objects are at hand, what sounds might impose themselves on the character, what sights might they react to?

Detective Shovel might be distracted by the flashing cop lights from outside and have to close a blind to focus, he could have to endure a boring conversation between two other cops lingering at the crime scene, he might recognize his favorite whiskey in the victim's collection and sneak a sip.

PART II

Drafting

In Part I you did the hard work of figuring out *what* to write. Great job! Now the only thing standing between you and that first draft of your scene is figuring out *how* you're going to write it.

"What do you mean, *how*? I've been writing for years!" Yes. But we're not talking thank-you notes, love letters, or essays for Professor Greene's course. Writing scripts is its own unique form of communication.

If you don't know it already, you'll soon see that the experience of reading a screenplay is a lot like the experience of watching a movie, which is pretty impressive if you think about it. Even though there's no way a script can capture every visual and auditory nuance for a fully produced film, somehow the minimalist, magical artistry of screenwriting can still convey that experience through words alone.

To accomplish this magic, you'll learn to deliver story information in an engaging way while adhering to the quirky specifics of the modern screenplay format.

Delivering story information, engaging your readers, and formatting effectively are the three pins that every scenewriter has to juggle. It may sound like a lot, but the following four chapters will walk you through every step.

Remember how at the beginning of Part I we said that it was too soon to write FADE IN? Well, guess what? By the end of Part II, you will have completed a properly formatted first draft.

5 The Fundamental Tools of Scenewriting

Imagine a person settling in to read your finished scene: they know nothing about your story, the location, or the characters. But word by word, line by line, you lead them into a world that you have created. You deliver a setting, a plot, and a tone—all the important story details they need to know what's happening, to empathize with your characters, and to understand their struggles.

Writing that story is an act of communication between you and the reader. And to communicate your story information, the two main tools you have available are *scene description* and *dialogue*. With these tools you will deliver information like where your scene takes place, who is there, what they want, what's stopping them from getting it, and what they do about it. Sound familiar? It should, because it's the awesome story stuff you worked so hard to figure out in Part I.

In tandem, these two powerful partners, scene description and dialogue, do the heavy narrative lifting in every script. This chapter introduces the basic mechanics of scene description and dialogue to get you going. In subsequent chapters we'll expand upon what you learn here.

Show 'Em What You Got

Scene description is that part of the screenplay where you capture the visual expression of your story. It is used to detail the setting, the characters that are present, and all the relevant things those characters do, see, and hear in the world around them. It is generally written in third-person, present tense. Here are three simple examples of unformatted[1] scene description:

---

[1] We will show you how to put everything in the proper script format in Chapter 8.

A rickety dark cabinet looms over the room.

Amelia watches the ducks swim by, oblivious to everyone around her.

The sound of a gunshot pierces the silence.

Writing scene description is very much like directing. Consider the cabinet that's called out in the first example. That line directs the reader's attention to the cabinet instead of the countless other details that would be visible in the same room. A reader could easily imagine a corresponding shot of the cabinet, influenced by the description—"dark," "rickety," "looms"—suggesting tension, suspense, or dread.

Cinema began as a purely visual medium. Indeed, movies used to be called "moving pictures." As a scenewriter working exclusively with words, it's easy to get caught up in language and forget just how much of your story can and will be communicated visually. Scene description is an opportunity to reconnect with—and make the most of—the visual manifestation of your story.

You have tremendous power and freedom in writing scene description, but you also have a major restriction. Unlike a novelist, who can peer into the inner thoughts of their characters or spend a few paragraphs detailing the backstory of a setting, you must stick with only what can be seen, heard, and inferred in the moment. In other words, your scene description needs to reflect what can be captured by a camera.[2]

Describing cabinets and raccoons and sunsets within the confines of this "camera capture" limitation is relatively straightforward. But when you need your reader to understand the internal state of a character, that can demand a little more effort. The good news is that in real life, everyone makes inferences from behavior and body language all the time: a kid stomping around is probably mad, a woman dancing down the street is probably feeling pretty good, and so on. As a scenewriter, you can tap into your lived experience to imagine what your character would do that's reflective of their emotions.

---

[2] This includes both picture and sound.

Consider the following two lines:

> Mary dreams of how fun it would be to kill her ex-boyfriend.

Versus:

> Mary grins and types into a search window, "How do I kill my ex?"

The first line requires an omniscient window into Mary's mind, so it fails the "camera capture" test. The second description, however, portrays actions that can be visualized and performed. Even though the two lines aren't perfectly equivalent, the second translates Mary's imaginings into filmable scene description to suggest her inner thoughts.

Let's think back to Kara, who wants to dance with Janelle. Your reader needs to know Kara's feelings for Janelle or the scene won't work. The problem is that her crush is an internal state of mind. If you want to express it through scene description, you must suggest it through actions, expressions, sound, and visual cues. Again, these are the things a camera can record.

Here are four of the infinite ways that scene description can point to the specific information that Kara is infatuated with Janelle:

> In a gym packed with hundreds of dancing kids, Kara only sees Janelle.

Or:

> Kara moves through a throng of dancers. She clumsily bumps into one. Looking up to apologize, she sees that it's Janelle, and melts on the spot.

Or:

> Kara scans the dance floor. She spots Janelle who is suddenly illuminated by a spotlight. Her dancing kicks into slow-motion, and the opening of Marvin Gaye's "Let's Get It On" spins over the gymnasium speakers.

Or:

> Kara watches Janelle dance. Beads of perspiration break out on Kara's forehead. Her heart pounds wildly, the sound of it fills the auditorium. Kara races to the refreshment table, chugs a cup of punch, and wipes the sweat from her brow. She glances back at Janelle still dancing, and lets out a low whistle.

None of the above examples explicitly says "Kara is infatuated with Janelle," yet they all imply it through a series of actions, reactions, performances, sound cues, music, and more. Moreover, the descriptions are all actable and filmable (with the last one requiring some interesting effects to showcase Kara's beating heart).

Note that complete sentences aren't a requirement. Scene description is evaluated on its effectiveness at communicating information, not its grammatical construction. Prioritize writing scene description that's efficient, clear, and evocative. Consider the following examples, which each use sentence fragments to quickly and efficiently describe what's happening.

QUEEN & SLIM by Lena Waithe, page 49:

> There's a row of about TWENTY WIGS.[3] They all come in different colors, lengths, and types. It looks like a museum in there. Queen walks by them. Touching a few. Smelling others. She's fascinated.

WALL-E by Andrew Stanton and Jim Reardon, page 29:

> Wally scans the concourse.
>
> Spots Eve's transport about to board a MONORAIL.

---

[3] Using allcaps is a great way to grab the reader's attention. We talk about this a lot more in Chapter 8.

He races after them.

Abandons the stunned John.

LADY BIRD by Greta Gerwig, page 75:

> It is <u>the</u> house. Danny's Grandmother's house. The blue one with the white shutters and the American Flag. The one Lady Bird said she lived in. Jenna is standing there in her uniform.

Pacing

Looking back at the examples of Kara's infatuation, all four deliver the same story information but with differing word counts. The last one, for example, is four times longer than the first.

You have a choice when it comes to writing scene description: you can make your point quickly and move on, or you can slow things down to emphasize something particularly important. As you'll see in the following chapters, time and attention are precious commodities so you'll want to spend your words wisely.

Let's go back to Betty, who left her purse behind at the club. Imagine that she has to get her purse back quickly so that she doesn't miss the last bus home. Compare the following two blocks of scene description communicating that Betty is in a hurry:

> Betty waits impatiently.

Versus:

> Betty stands in line. She taps her foot. She puts her hands on her hips. She checks her phone. The line doesn't move. She lets out a long sigh.

The world seems to slow to a crawl when you're in a rush. The latter description captures that experience by literally slowing down the reader to make the point. It's fun to read because it never explicitly says that Betty is impatient; it implies it and leaves the conclusion up to the reader.[4] But is her impatience important enough to the story that we should spend so many words on it? Does the extra emphasis on her impatience pay off? Or will the script be just as good, if not better, if it makes the "impatient" point quickly and moves on?

It may be fun to write flavorful, poetic prose. It can be fun to read it, too. But agents, managers, producers, actors, directors, and all the other folks you want to read your script are busy people. If your scene description is slow and laborious everywhere, they'll drop it in a hot minute. So focus on the key information that propels your story forward and zip quickly through everything else.

Let's look at some examples from produced scripts to see how scene description can be used to deliver expository information in practice.

On page 13 of GET OUT by Jordan Peele, Chris and Rose have just hit something with their car:

> Rose gets out of her car and inspects the damage. Chris gets out as well. There's a small bloody dent in the hood.

Peele keeps the scene description crisp and clear. There's no unbuckling of seat belts, no pulling on door handles, no description of the asphalt underfoot, or the nearby flora. Instead, he describes only the essential actions so that he can skip to the good stuff (discovering what they hit, and the consequences of it).

On page 63 of LADY BIRD, Gerwig describes Jenna's house with wonderful efficiency:

> A fancy McMansion, giant but not utterly tasteless. A low-key house party. Lady Bird wanders through the palatial house, looking for Jenna.

Instead of calling out specific architectural or furnishing details, Gerwig leverages a few choice adjectives to paint a picture of the massive home and

---

[4] A subject we cover in detail in the next chapter.

the party going on within as seen through Lady Bird's eyes. Even seemingly important details—like who else is there or the decor—are left out. All that matters at this moment is Lady Bird's goal and the setting.

On page 79 of MOONLIGHT, writer Barry Jenkins chronicles Black driving to Miami:

> An extended beat of this traveling, of the road and trees and wind, the speed of the passing land and soundscape escalating, building, the whole of it coalescing into a hypnotic rhythm, then...
>
> WAVES
>
> ...both the sight and sound of waves crashing, lashing at the shore.

The story information delivered in these lines is that Black takes a trance-inducing drive that finally ends at the ocean. The reader is clued in to the importance of this moment for Black because Jenkins takes his time with it. He does some heavy tonal work here too, showing just how powerful scene description can be at communicating mood in addition to information.

EXERCISE: Basic Practice with Scene Description

The best way to understand how scene description works is to read scripts. Seriously. As soon as possible, and as many as you can find. That's why the first part of this exercise is to find a script for a film or series you admire and read at least the first five pages. Be sure to read an actual script (and not a transcript). If you want suggestions, grab one from the appendix. And read the whole thing if you have the time. It will be worth it.

If this is your first time reading a script, you may be confused by unfamiliar shorthand like "EXT. BASEBALL STADIUM—DAY." Don't worry too much about that stuff right now; we'll cover the essentials of formatting in Chapter 8. Instead, focus on the scene description.

Watch how the writer directs your attention while limiting description to what can be seen or heard in the moment. Try to translate the lines you read into the story information that's delivered: what characters want, why, what's in their way, and what they do to circumvent their obstacles. Also take note of how the tone is imparted through word choice.

When you're done getting a feel for how another screenwriter approaches scene description, it's time for you to get a little practice. Start by writing a single line that describes where your scene unfolds. Use the third-person and present tense. Feel free to model it after something you read in the script. It can be as simple as:

> This is a busy club.

Almost every scene will have one or more characters present. So next, write a line of scene description to establish your main character and what they are doing.

> Betty stands outside waiting to get in.

Next, pick an action that your character will take in your scene and try to write it as succinctly as possible in scene description.

> She skips to the front of the line.

Now examine the language you employed in your three lines of scene description. What words have you used to capture the tone and mood of your scene? Does someone walk or do they dance, prance, strut, or glide? Is the ceiling high or is it towering, majestic, or dizzying?

Rewrite your three lines with an eye towards tone. Add flavor with strategic choice of verbs and adjectives, such as:

> The Quaking Palm is thumping. Betty fumes while waiting to get in. She rudely shoulders her way to the front of the line.

Finally, write a new version of the same events where you slow down the pacing in order to stretch time. Think back to the examples of Kara discovering Janelle on the dance floor. Linger on the moment-to-moment actions, breaking them into smaller steps as a way to explore this more cinematic approach to conveying information. Don't forget to consider sound as well as visual elements. Let your imagination run wild!

Use Your Words

Dialogue is that part of the script that captures the words your characters speak. For now, indicate dialogue by writing a character's name in allcaps followed by a colon and then whatever words they say.[5] For example:

> MEI: Wow. Creepy cabinet.

> EARL: Are those ducks?

> SHAWNA: Please tuck in your shirt.

In addition to the spoken words themselves, written dialogue can also capture things like pauses, interruptions, emphasis, and volume changes that occur in typical conversations. It's easy to do this through punctuation and formatting.

Italics, bold, allcaps, and underlining are all ways to indicate vocal emphasis. In general, ellipses signal a hesitation. Dashes generally represent interruption in the form of two hyphens at the end of a block of dialogue, though as you'll see later (Chapter 8) you have a lot of leeway in how you use both pauses and interruptions. What matters most is that your intention is clear.

Consider how punctuation and formatting adds naturalistic pauses, interruptions, and emphasis into the following exchange:

> BETTY: Excuse me, I left my purse inside... Can I please run in and grab—

> BOUNCER: Back of the line, lady.

> BETTY: You don't *understand*... I don't want to stay, it's just—

---

[5] You'll do this differently when you learn the screenplay format in Chapter 8.

BOUNCER: There's a line for a reason—

BETTY: I NEED MY PURSE!

BOUNCER: Sure. And I need my job.

This exchange also demonstrates how powerful dialogue can be in delivering critical story information. The first thing to notice is Betty's scene goal. Though people don't always come right out and say what they want directly, in the dialogue above Betty says it explicitly:

BETTY: Excuse me, I left my purse inside. . . Can I please run in and grab—

When taking a first pass at your scene dialogue, it can be helpful to state what the character wants in simple, straightforward terms like this. You can complicate things later by adding subtext, preoccupations, dialect, and other complexities that we'll cover in Chapter 11, but getting your character's goal out in the open allows the scene to move forward with the reader fully informed about who wants what.

The very next spoken line in the example establishes the obstacle. The Bouncer is directly the way of Betty getting what she wants:

BETTY: Excuse me, I left my purse inside. . . Can I please run in and grab—

BOUNCER: Back of the line, lady.

In terms of motivation, Betty's is pretty clear. After all, who wouldn't want their purse back? But why is the Bouncer putting up such a fuss? Readers need to understand the reason that he opposes Betty in order for the Bouncer to be more than one-dimensional and for their conflict to be convincing. Again, this information emerges directly from dialogue:

BETTY: I NEED MY PURSE!

BOUNCER: Sure. And I need my job.

The Bouncer's opposition isn't random: letting her in could cost him his job, and this grounds him for the reader as a believable (and relatable) obstacle.

Just a few lines of dialogue are all it takes to quickly and clearly establish two distinct characters with different—and mutually opposing—goals.

What other information comes across in their exchange? Betty's first attempt to get what she wants is a polite request. This strategy offers a glimpse into her character. When she is rebuffed, it provides a chance to see how she will change her tactics. In this case, Betty assumes that she isn't getting what she wants because she hasn't made herself clear. She tries again. Finally, aware that she's being stonewalled, she gets desperate.

If we were to continue the dialogue, what would come next? Betty has tried clarifying her objective without success, so, following our model from Part I, she would need to change course and try a new approach. Maybe she'd plead with the Bouncer, maybe she'd browbeat, maybe she'd try to bribe him. Whatever she tries, each new attempt will convey new information about Betty to the reader. And each rejection will provide new information about the bouncer.

Fundamentally, characters speak for the same reason that they act: in order to get what they want. From a baby crying for milk to a Senator intoning, "We must impeach this President," talking is often the most efficient way they can affect change. Check out the following examples of dialogue and how they quickly establish mutually exclusive character desires.

Here's an exchange from page 39 of QUEEN & SLIM:

> SLIM: I don't think it's smart for us to be walking into gas stations.
>
> QUEEN: It's not that scary. I told you what to do.
>
> SLIM: You only saying that cause you don't have to do it.
>
> QUEEN: You got this. I believe in you.

SLIM: Don't patronize me.

QUEEN: I'm not.

As a fugitive, Slim doesn't want to risk being seen in a gas station, but Queen wants him to go pay for gas—mutually opposing goals.

On page 88 of LADY BIRD, Lady Bird is trying on dresses. Her mother is "helping."

LADY BIRD: Why can't you say I look nice?

MARION: I thought you didn't even care what I think.

LADY BIRD: I still want you to think I look good.

MARION: I'm sorry, I was telling you the truth. Do you want me to lie?

Notice how Lady Bird states in explicit terms what she wants: for her mother to say she looks nice. But Marion wants her to choose a different dress and isn't capable of putting aside her opinions to give her daughter what she wants.

On page 17 of JOJO RABBIT by Taika Waititi, Jojo and his mother discuss leaving the house for the first time since Jojo's grenade accident:

JOJO: I don't want to go out there.

ROSIE: Don't be silly, of course you do.

JOJO: I look stupid. People will stare.

ROSIE: Let them! Enjoy the attention, kid. Not everyone is lucky enough to look stupid.

The reader understands that Jojo is too embarrassed to go outside, and also that his mother wants to get him out of the house. Notice in this instance that Rosie stands as an obstacle to what Jojo wants, even though they are allies in the wider story.

EXERCISE: Basic Practice with Dialogue

It was true with scene description; it's also true with dialogue: the more you read, the more you'll learn. So read at least five more pages of a script—the same one you read before is fine—and this time pay attention to how the writer communicates story information through dialogue. In particular, try to identify what characters want, why they want it, what's stopping them, and what they're doing about it.

Let's follow your reading with a little dialogue practice. Select something that your main character wants to achieve in your scene, such as: to go home, to catch the train, to get the last piece of pie, to quiet their annoying uncle, etc. Write a line of dialogue that expresses that goal as clearly as possible. For example:

> BETTY: I forgot my purse inside the club and I would like to get it back.

> SISTER: I'm taking the last bagel.

> PILOT: Please tell me you have the correct coordinates.

Here you've put the exposition of what your character wants directly into the words they say.

Now you're going to expand this into a brief dialogue with a second character. Who is your character speaking with? Give them an opposing goal and a reason for having it, and express that information in what they say.

> BETTY: I forgot my purse inside the club and I would like to get it back.

> BOUNCER: I need to keep my job.

> SISTER: I'm taking the last bagel.

> BROTHER: Any chance I could have half?

PILOT: Please tell me you have the correct coordinates.

CO-PILOT: I wish I could.

Finally, let's get you started working with interruptions and pauses to add some naturalism into your information-laden dialogue. Expand your conversation to four lines. Have your main character respond but get interrupted, and sneak in a pause somewhere too. For example:

BETTY: I forgot my purse inside the club and I would like to get it back.

BOUNCER: I need to keep my job.

BETTY: You think letting me back inside is going to—

BOUNCER: Look. . . do I need Sammy here to show you the back of the line?

SISTER: I'm taking the last bagel.

BROTHER: Any chance I could have half?

SISTER: You went to the store and you KNEW we needed more—

BROTHER: How about. . . half of a half?

PILOT: Please tell me you have the correct coordinates.

CO-PILOT: I wish I could.

PILOT: How about you call in to air-traffic control?

CO-PILOT: Sorry, friend, not my job.

6 The Art of Reader Engagement

Like anyone who is drawn to writing scripts, you have undoubtedly experienced many unforgettable moments on screen. It doesn't matter if these scenes were from horror films, tear-jerkers, comedies, documentaries, or thrillers. They stayed with you because they were captivating.

The last chapter discussed the basics of how to deliver story information, and while those basics are essential to writing great scenes, they're not the whole ballgame. A great scene doesn't just deliver story information to readers, it absorbs their full attention and emotions. It's transformative, compelling, captivating, and unignorable. In our terms, a great scene *engages the reader*.

An engaged reader is going to laugh out loud, jump in surprise, cry, think, and draw connections. An engaged reader wonders what's going on and what's coming next, how your character is going to get out of a jam, and what will happen if and when they do. An engaged reader keeps reading because they feel that they must. It's an itch that they need to scratch.

This chapter details four techniques you can use to engage your reader. Get to know them all, and you'll be able to transform your writing from functional to captivating.

Make 'Em Work for It

A wonderful way of hooking your reader's interest is to paint an incomplete picture of what is happening, thereby leaving them to fill in the gaps. In other words, instead of telling your reader everything they need to know, you lead them in the right direction by dropping successive clues. Their reward comes when their close attention reveals the right conclusion. It's kind of like constructing a *treasure hunt* that they need to solve in order to make sense of your scene.

What does this look like in practice? Consider the following:

> Giannis is a busboy at the Athena Diner. He secretly carries a kitten in the pocket of his apron and, as he clears tables, feeds her fries left behind by customers.

That's a brief and clear introduction. But it also tells the reader everything they need to know without asking them to do any work. It's no more engaging than an instruction manual because it doesn't give the reader a way of participating in the discovery of information. Giannis snuck a kitten into work and is feeding her leftover fries, for crying out loud! Can't we do something more engaging with that?

Indeed we can. A treasure hunt, by contrast, will bring the reader in as a participant by making them work for the important story information. Compare the above description with the following:

> Old fries litter a Formica table. A rag sweeps them onto a plate.
>
> As Giannis carries it to the kitchen he hears a quiet mewling. He looks left and right, then grabs a french fry and holds it near his apron pocket. The tiny head of a kitten pops out, grabs the fry, and disappears. Giannis resumes his work.

The clues we offer in this case are specific images that add up to the information we want to convey. The mewling, Giannis's suspicious behavior, the fry being held near his apron all hint at the conclusion that is paid off when the kitten rears its head.

The strategy works because of an unwritten contract between the reader and writer. Before any scene begins, there's an underlying expectation that the scene will consist of something more than random events and dialogue. In other words, no matter what actions, images, and sounds you conjure up for your scene, your reader expects that they will soon cohere into a meaningful, complete picture. What's awesome about this dynamic is that the writer can leverage the reader's curiosity. It's like they're primed to be engaged in the story before they've even read a word.

Using this approach, you may notice that this scene description doesn't start on Giannis. Rather, action develops from an image—fries on a table—that needs further explanation. Opening a scene with an *unexplained image* is a terrific way to set up a little question. The question (what do fries have to do with anything?) is addressed in the next line (Aha! Someone is clearing them). But that, too, asks a question: who is it? In fact, a careful reading shows that each line of scene description in the example adds another hint to what is happening by posing a new question to the reader. Note that this approach of leading the reader into the scene bit by bit is basically the opposite of writing an establishing shot.

To send your reader on a treasure hunt, you have to translate whatever information you need to convey into a series of clues. No single clue will give the final answer but, when sequenced together by an attentive reader, they will paint a full and clear picture of what's going on. Any and all of the Part I information that's in your scene—characters, goals, obstacles, locations, etc.—can be set up using this approach.

Dialogue can be used for treasure hunts too. If the writer drops the reader into a conversation that is already taking place, the reader is forced to play catch up. The reader's curiosity again hooks them into the story, prompting them to make connections in order to make sense of the situation. Imagine if the following was the first moment of a scene in which Giannis is clearing tables:

CUSTOMER: Did you hear that?

GIANNIS: Hear what?

CUSTOMER: Sounded like a kitten.

GIANNIS: Probably just the A/C kicking in.

CUSTOMER: Hey, is your apron pocket moving?

GIANNIS: Sorry, I gotta get these to the kitchen—

To further demonstrate this idea of a treasure hunt, below are three scripted moments that suggest—but do not explicitly name—easily describable situations. The full meaning is left for the reader to figure out by following the clues.

1

A bell rings. Brady throws his bicycle onto a rack and dashes towards the building. He races down an empty corridor and flings open a door. Rows of students look up from their silent writing as Brady sheepishly walks to his desk.

2

CARLY: Next week?

DAD: Do you really think next week would be different?

CARLY: How about Tuesday? Right after school.

DAD: Don't you have track?

CARLY: Please? I hate shots.

DAD: It'll be over in five minutes.

CARLY: Next week. Please. I'll get two shots. All the shots.

DAD: Just the one vaccine will be fine.

3

A limousine pulls up in front of the courthouse. Humphrey steps out, dressed to the nines. While walking up the steps he is joined by Miranda.

MIRANDA: Nice ride—

HUMPHREY: Can we please get this over with?

MIRANDA: —I took the subway.

HUMPHREY: You're a regular woman of the people.

MIRANDA: I suppose you're trying to spend every last dollar of mine while you can, is that it?

HUMPHREY: How about you save it for the judge?

Hopefully it wasn't too hard for you to come to your own conclusions about what is going on in each example. In all three scenarios there are multiple hints to follow that slowly lead the reader to a clear understanding of the circumstances.

The process is a little like handing the reader a jumble of jigsaw puzzle pieces without telling them what the pieces will look like when fitted together. If the first pieces you offer are solid green, they might not be able to conclude anything. But add some brown, a piece with dark eyes, a few that add up to a mane, a tail, hooves, and eventually they're looking at a horse grazing on a grassy hill.

Treasure hunts are useful everywhere. They are particularly common at the start of scenes and larger stories when the reader necessarily has to learn where the action is taking place, who is involved, and what's going on. Consider the following examples of treasure hunts that come from scenes near the beginning of feature scripts:

On page 1 of MOONLIGHT, Jenkins suggests that Juan is the head of a drug operation through a number of small clues in both dialogue and scene description.

Juan cuts his engine, exits the car and begins across the street. The boys tense up as Juan approaches, make room as he continues all the way over to the brick wall behind them.

JUAN: Business good?

One of the boys, TERRENCE (18, dreadlocks and rail thin), bows his chest to speak.

TERRENCE: Business good. Everybody cleaned out, it's in the cut if you want it.

Juan just nodding his head, looking at the ground stretching before them, kind of day where phosphorous fumes wave above the asphalt.

JUAN: Hold on to that, register don't empty til' the weekend, feel me?

Terrence nodding, the other boys' heads bowed slightly, a hierarchy here.

On page 7 of GET OUT, Peele hints, without saying explicitly, that Chris and Rose are going on a trip to meet Rose's family.

Chris packs a small bag of luggage. Rose lays on the bed.

ROSE: Toothbrush. . . Deodorant. . .

CHRIS: Check. . . Check. . . .

Chris puts a cigarette in his mouth. Rose pops up and grabs the cigarette from his mouth and breaks it. Chris tries to feign incredulousness but is amused.

CHRIS: I'm not gonna have one the whole weekend.

ROSE: You quit, remember?

CHRIS: I'm nervous.

ROSE: Why? They're going to love you.

CHRIS: Yeah? How do you know?

ROSE: Let's see, you're smart, sweet, handsome, creative. . . You're you.

CHRIS: Good answer.

On page 2 of BOOKSMART, writers Halpern & Haskins, Fogel, and Silberman drop clues about how much Amy and Molly have hated high school. Their game-like attempt to one-up each other further hints to the reader just how close they are, too.

> They pass an EMOTIONAL GIRL crying with her friends—
>
> EMOTIONAL GIRL: I mean these were the best four years of our lives!
>
> Molly gives Amy a look.
>
> MOLLY: Can you imagine a world in which these were actually the best four years of our lives?
>
> AMY: Maybe if I immediately lost all my limbs, and my eyesight and hearing, and I was just like a human potato. I'd be like, "remember when I had my limbs and could see and hear? Those were the best four years."
>
> MOLLY: Or if I was convicted of a crime I didn't commit and spent the rest of my life in a Thai prison.
>
> AMY: If I spent the rest of my life reading in the backseat of a car.
>
> MOLLY: You do get so carsick.

EXERCISE: Mapping out a Treasure Hunt

Choose a specific piece of information that you need to deliver to the reader in your scene. For example, you could choose something like who the main character is, where the scene is located, or the obstacle.

Now construct hints about this piece of information for your reader to follow. Create dots to connect; puzzle pieces to assemble. Brainstorm three or more clues that add up to a concrete piece of information. Start with the most inconclusive image, line of dialogue, or sound and work your way towards the more specific. Once you have some clues in mind, write the lines of scene description and/or dialogue that you need to set up the treasure hunt.

Reread what you have written. Do your clues add up to the information that you meant to convey at the point you expect your reader to have figured it out? Or do they point to an incorrect or ambiguous conclusion? If the latter, keep adding details until you're sure that the hints lead the reader exactly where you want them to go.

Nobody Expects the Spanish Inquisition!

Another great way to grab your reader's attention is to establish an expectation about what will happen in your scene and then undermine it. The setup could involve work you explicitly do in the scene, or it can be based upon common assumptions the reader brings to the table. In either case, your job, as the writer, is to lead the reader in a specific direction, only to knock them off balance. But like a joke, you have to save the punchline—aka the unexpected twist—for the end.

Tons of on-screen gags use this setup/punchline approach. Here's one from page 3 of MOONRISE KINGDOM by Wes Anderson and Roman Coppola:

> SCOUT MASTER WARD: Roosevelt. How's that lanyard coming?
>
> ROOSEVELT (Frustrated): I don't know. I think I skipped a stitch.
>
> INSERT: A small, woven, multi-colored cord with a rabbit's foot attached to the end of it. It has been braided exceedingly badly and is brutally twisted and misshapen.

The writers set up Roosevelt's line to establish the expectation that the lanyard is just a little bit off (setup), then reveal it to be a horrible mess (punchline).

Conversely, you can also lead the reader to expect failure, only to surprise them with unanticipated success. This happens time and again in SCOTT PILGRIM VS. THE WORLD, written by Edgar Wright & Michael Bacall, such as on page 19:

SCOTT: Do you know this one girl with hair like this?

Scott sketches an incomprehensible drawing of Ramona.

COMEAU: Yeah man. Ramona Flowers.

No way that should have worked. And yet…

Your readers will automatically have expectations about your scene even if you don't explicitly set them up, because they've been around. They know what birthday parties are like, they know what goes on in classrooms, at family dinners, in court, or in any of the countless generic settings and activities that make up "real" life on screen.

If you drop them into one of those familiar situations and give them exactly what they expect, then you aren't exploiting the full potential of your writing to engage and are going to lose your readers. Upending their expectations, however, will keep them engaged and on their toes.

Consider the following:

Mourners are gathered at a solemn, well-attended funeral.

ARCHIE is trying really, really hard not to laugh.

Almost anyone's assumptions about typical behavior at a funeral would be upended by Archie's suppressed laughter. His unexpected behavior sets up a question: Why is Archie acting in this surprising way? Wanting to know the answer to that question will pull the reader deeper into the script.

Here's another example of upended expectations at a funeral:

A solemn, well-attended funeral.

PRIEST: We will always remember Bridget. She was the most special chinchilla.

Not the typical funeral, so that's fun and unusual. But still a bummer for Bridget.

Here's a great example of deliberate misdirection on the first page of the script for WALL-E:

> A range of mountains takes form in the haze.
>
> Moving closer.
>
> The mountains are piles of TRASH.
>
> The entire surface is nothing but waste.

The opening view of the mountain range suggests a bucolic panorama, but is quickly revealed to be quite the opposite. Reading lines like this is like watching an expert magician's sleight of hand. It's satisfying to be entertained by someone who's showing you only and exactly what they want you to see at the moment.

Here are a few more examples of scenes that engage by upending reader expectations.

Page 34 of GET OUT features multiple small little surprises, including this one:

> Rose and Chris make hushed love in her bed. A stuffed lion seems to watch Chris. He turns it away.

The stuffed lion seems to come from left field. After all, the first line of scene description is about their lovemaking, so the image of the lion shows up quite unexpectedly. But upon reflection, they are in Rose's childhood room, so it does make sense that her childhood friends would be around. Indeed, it signals how Chris is fully immersed in—and distracted by—the weirdness that is Rose's family.

On page 4 of BOOKSMART, Molly and Amy approach Principal Brown about budget numbers for next year. But instead of applauding his star students for being on top of things and ushering them into his office as anyone might expect...

> He starts <u>slowly closing the door</u>.

PRINCIPAL BROWN: Let's just focus on getting through the rest of the day without anything horrible happening, okay?

MOLLY: I'm sorry, are you shutting the door on us? This isn't subtle. You can't just close the door. We will persist—

He shuts it in their faces.

Even Molly is surprised!

On page 85 of QUEEN & SLIM, Junior is standing up to a cop as part of a peaceful protest:

JUNIOR: I have a right to protest.

BLACK POLICE OFFICER: I understand that, but you don't have a permit. So that means you're breaking the law.

JUNIOR: What you gon do, kill me?

BLACK POLICE OFFICER: No, but I will arrest you.

The Police Officer LIFTS UP THE BULLETPROOF SHIELD ON HIS HELMET so there's one less barrier between them.

BLACK POLICE OFFICER: I'm begging you. Go home.

The Police Officer GRABS Junior by his arms—in an attempt to calm him down. But he wrestles free.

Junior pulls out a SMALL HAND GUN. He aims it at the only part of the Officer's body that's not covered.

He SHOOTS him in the face. Causing the Officer's head to EXPLODE IN HIS HELMET.

Junior's violence is a startling and unexpected turn, though upon reflection it is perfectly in line with his politics.

Shock

You can also upend your reader's expectations by making unanticipated stuff happen to and/or around your character. Make them respond to a surprise thrown their way, and your reader will be engaged with the ride that follows.

Take a wedding. Readers will expect a happy couple, fine attire, family, speeches, and dancing. Land a UFO by the buffet or have a dragon explode out of the cake, and you'll shock the reader out of their preconceived expectations.

But you need to be careful with these kinds of shocks. Sure, they'll snap your reader to attention, but to keep them engaged, the new element has to relate in some way to the larger story you're telling. In other words, if you throw a completely random element into your story as a cheap stab at engagement, it will likely leave your readers unsatisfied in the end.

> In AVATAR: THE LAST AIRBENDER (book 2 episode 4), the gang is knocked off their course by a sudden, unexplained whirlwind. This completely unpredictable surprise forces them to crash in a swamp where they struggle to reunite and escape. But, as they learn during their journey through the swamp, the whirlwind brought them there for a reason. And that explanation ultimately makes the initial shock of the whirlwind satisfying.

EXERCISE: Leverage the Unusual in Your Scene

Identify one or more moments in your scene where you have the potential to upend your reader's expectations about what will happen. As a reminder, this process involves establishing an expectation (or relying on a preexisting one), then delivering something different instead.

A good way to mine for this kind of material is to identify the things about your characters, your world, and/or the situation in your scene that are somewhat askew from the "real world" because that's where your readers' implicit expectations can easily be overturned.

A few areas to consider are:

Setting: What's special about this place? Is it just a stereotypical version of the setting or can you give it some unexpected personality instead?

Actions/Dialogue: Is there an opportunity for one or more of your characters to act or speak in a way that subverts the norm? Like a teacher's pet disrupting class, a frail grandmother winning a fistfight, or a jock reciting poetry?

Outcomes: Can you set up the expectation that your character will succeed in their attempt, but have them fail miserably instead? Or have them make an inane attempt, doomed for failure, that actually works?

Events: Does something disruptive and shocking happen in your scene, and if so, can you use the timing of that reveal to your benefit? How does it relate to the main character and their journey?

Choose one of the above areas, or another of your own, and do the work of setting up the reader's expectation only to deliver a punchline that upends it. It need not be a major twist or turn; small reveals are compelling and engaging too!

Make 'Em Wait

You've bought your ticket and popcorn, found your seat, and the film is about to begin. It's supposed to be the scariest screamfest since THE BABADOOK, and with the first shot of a lovely tree-lined street you already begin to feel the hairs rising on the back of your neck.

You see a woman in the living room of a Victorian house, reading a novel, sipping a glass of Chardonnay, a baby sleeping peacefully in its crib beside her, when suddenly she hears a strange clicking coming from the basement. "Kitty?" she whispers aloud. She listens. There it is again. She gets up and looks down the darkened staircase. Funny, the lights won't switch on. "Kitty?" she asks again. And you scream to yourself, "It's not the cat! Are you crazy?!" She puts a foot on the first step. "Grab the baby and get out!" But does she listen? No!

She doesn't know she's in a horror film, but we do. We feel the fear she doesn't even know she should have. We know there's something terrifying coming at some point in this picture. It might be now, it might be later. But it's definitely coming.

It's the same relationship that the audience has when watching Charlie Chaplin drop a banana peel onto a crowded street, or seeing the ticking time bomb placed in the back of a car in the opening shot of Hitchcock's TOUCH OF EVIL, or a screwdriver floating on a collision course towards the space station in GRAVITY. In those examples, we're eagerly anticipating the moment when someone slips on the peel, we're waiting on pins and needles for someone to find that bomb before it explodes, and we're wondering what the heck is going to happen when the wrench hits the space station.

All of these examples leverage the same trick for engagement: they set events on a collision course and then make us wait... and wait... and wait for the impact. The reader *anticipates* what will happen. This technique is more familiarly known as *suspense*.

The examples above all feature characters who know less than the audience. You can also use anticipation when the reader and the character know the same things. Imagine the following:

> Kai slowly ascends the damp ladder one hand after the other. She's worried.
>
> She reaches the top of the high platform and looks down.
>
> The pool looms. A million miles away. Empty and waiting for her.
>
> Her mom waves from the stands, a tiny speck.
>
> Kai pales.

In this case, the anticipated collision is one between Kai and the water. The readers are right there with Kai, wondering what is going to happen. Will she take the scary leap, or faint, or turn around and sheepishly climb down? The suspense of this situation comes—appropriately—from the writer *suspending* the answer for a while. If you take the time to set something like this up, you don't want to rush the resolution. Make 'em wait! Let the reader suffer along with Kai.

The engaging part for the reader is the anticipation. If you set up the inevitability of a dramatic event, the reader will stick around to see it unfold. It's the writer's choice to either give it to them straight (Kai jumps and we hear her screaming as she plummets to the water and lands with a sickening splash) or give them an unexpected result (Kai jumps and twirls gracefully before nailing a perfectly splashless entry.). But in all events, the anticipation needs to be paid off with the collision.

Here are some example scenes that leverage anticipation for reader engagement:

In a scene from GAME OF THRONES (s5e1), Daenerys visits her two dragons who are locked in a massive underground cell. Because of heavy lifting done by the writers in this and earlier episodes of the show, the audience knows that Daenerys is second-guessing her choice to chain up her dragons. They are her children, after all, and she loves them. But they're still dragons, and they're getting bigger, and she's rightfully terrified of them. The 90-second scene of Daenerys walking the lengths of the dungeon is driven entirely by suspense. It puts the audience right with Daenerys, feeling her anticipation and concern as she walks deeper into the murky depths, uncertain of what she will find.

In a scene from THE WAY WAY BACK, the main character Duncan says goodbye to his summer friends from the water park by attempting to pass another rider on the waterslide (a feat never before completed, according to park lore). No one knows if the risky maneuver will succeed. Duncan enters at the top of the covered slide, and we wait, wondering at the outcome. When they finally pop out at the end... well, you should really read for yourself what happens.

At the graduation party in BOOKSMART, Molly has been super flirty with her crush, Nick. She expects that they'll hook up, a long-term goal she has been pursuing throughout a good portion of the script. But readers know from a previous scene that Nick was kissing someone else at the party. The reader anticipates that Molly will be devastated when she finds out. But the inevitable collision is suspended for an entire scene before the truth unfolds.

EXERCISE: Setting Up Anticipation

Even if your scene doesn't naturally suggest a collision, this exercise is an opportunity to consider this engagement strategy and to get some practice thinking about constructing one.

The plot of our scene with Kara and Janelle is fundamentally designed around a collision. We know Kara wants to dance with Janelle. When she finally makes her move to ask, the reader anticipates the result and is on the journey with her step by step.

But even a scene like Betty and the bouncer can include a collision. Imagine that Betty has been conclusively rebuffed by the bouncer. As she retreats, she sees a lead pipe by the side of the road. She considers, then picks it up and starts marching deliberately back to the bouncer. Just like that: a collision is imminent! Is she really going to use this pipe on the guy?!

In both of these cases, we are with the main character as they act. We know and see only what they know and see. But you can also position the reader ahead of a character to create suspense. Being ahead of a character means that the reader has more knowledge about a character's circumstances than the character does. Imagine our scene with Detective Shovel. What if, as he enters the crime scene, we know in advance that the criminal has set up a boobytrap? If he opens the refrigerator, that'll be it for our hero. In this example we will follow his moves in anticipation of the deadly appliance.

In each of these hypothetical cases the writer has set up a collision and the outcome could resolve in one of many ways. Will it work out well, or will it end badly? There's at least one result in each example that's painful to consider, one that we hope doesn't happen for our character. Getting your reader to feel that emotion feeds the suspense.

It's like a pop fly at a Little League baseball game. With the crack of the bat, everyone's heads look up. We know that ball is going to come down, right? If the next thing you show is the distracted center fielder playing with butterflies in the grass, you've set up a nice moment of anticipation for your reader. There are multiple possible outcomes—which will it be?

Find an opportunity in your scene where you can set something into motion that won't be resolved for a beat, something where the resolution is inevitable, undetermined, and might end badly for your character. It doesn't have to be a life-or-death situation; it could be as simple as a pull/push door encounter with public embarrassment on the line. Try setting up that collision in scene description and/or dialogue, and then milk it for a beat so that your reader can enjoy the anticipatory suspense.

Feast Your Eyes on This!

The final of our four methods to engage your reader is to present them with an unforgettable bit of *spectacle*. We're talking things that are straight-up beautiful, terrifying, unbelievable, mesmerizing, horrific, or otherwise viscerally gripping. As long as it's integral to your story, you can serve your reader whatever eye candy you can dream up.

Spectacle can take all kinds of forms. There are breathtaking setpieces like the Emerald City in THE WIZARD OF OZ, the floating alien ships in DISTRICT 9 or ARRIVAL, the Death Star in STAR WARS, and the diverse, animal-filled city of ZOOTOPIA.

There are moments where characters behave in incredible, superhuman ways. Consider Trinity running on a wall in THE MATRIX, the gorgeous tree-top martial arts of CROUCHING TIGER, HIDDEN DRAGON, and Legolas single-handedly taking down a giant beast in THE LORD OF THE RINGS: THE RETURN OF THE KING.

You can leverage spectacle to present your readers something unusual or uncanny that's unique to your story's world. There's the enchanted ambulatory structure that is HOWL'S MOVING CASTLE, King Kong climbing the Empire State Building, and Thanos snapping his fingers to kill billions in AVENGERS: INFINITY WAR.

Spectacle can also include macabre and horrific displays that are hard to forget like the flogging scene in 12 YEARS A SLAVE, the dead security guard that Hannibal Lecter dresses like an angel in THE SILENCE OF THE LAMBS, the devastating attack on Omaha Beach in SAVING PRIVATE RYAN, or the grim battle of the bastards in GAME OF THRONES.

Writing spectacle is about translating your unusual vision into words for the reader so they can imagine it for themselves.

On page 45 of SCOTT PILGRIM VS. THE WORLD, readers are treated to the spectacular entrance of Ramona's first Angry Ex:

> Sex Bob-omb rock out, barely into the first verse when a chunk of ceiling CRASHES down and a SPINDLY INDIAN HIPSTER KID DIVES HEAD FIRST through the hole, finger pointed at Scott as he sails towards the stage!

On page 59 of THE INCREDIBLES, writer Brad Bird captures the beauty and high-tech sophistication of Syndrome's island lair, as seen through Bob's eyes:

> The MONOPOD zooms along a track which rises from a tunnel beneath the lagoon and sweeps through the jungle. Although this is his second time here, Bob is seeing the island with new eyes. It is a WONDER.
>
> The monopod track disappears straight into a rushing WATERFALL. Suddenly the waterfall PARTS, the water separating like an enormously long chiffon curtain, revealing the intricately designed architecture hidden underneath.

Spectacle need not be *that* spectacular, as long as it is presented as such. On page 57 of Alan Ball's script AMERICAN BEAUTY, for example, spectacle comes through in the most unexpected of places: a plastic bag, blowing in the wind:

> On VIDEO: We're in an empty parking lot on a cold, gray day. Something is floating across from us... it's an empty, wrinkled, white PLASTIC BAG.
>
> We follow it as the wind carries it in a circle around us, sometimes whipping it about violently, or, without warning, sending it soaring skyward, then letting it float gracefully down to the ground...

EXERCISE: Add a Little Wonder

You may or may not have an obvious place to leverage spectacle in your scene, but in considering the possibility you may stumble upon a wonderful option that you wouldn't have otherwise considered.

Think about all the building blocks of your scene and contemplate each one as an opportunity for spectacle. Can the set be jaw-dropping? Even something as simple as a water fountain can be written into a dazzling, magical oasis. Might you be able to take one of your character actions and elevate it into something sublime for your reader? Could you turn a walk into a dance, or an argument into a choreographed fight? Is there an object or event in your scene that is unusual and thus ripe for deeper visual exploration?

Spectacle is often the place for exaggeration, so let yourself go wild. Choose something in your scene and enhance or elaborate it to the level of the beautiful, unbelievable, uncanny, or repulsive.

7 The Unformatted Draft

Now it's time to pull together everything you've learned so far and write an *unformatted draft* of your scene. As the name implies, in writing an unformatted draft you don't have to worry about the peculiarities of the quirky screenplay format (those come in Chapter 8) and can instead focus on storytelling.

This is exciting stuff. By the end of this chapter you will have the first rendering of your scene from beginning to end, complete with characters acting and talking.

The unformatted draft has a lot in common with other documents you may have heard about, such as *outlines* and *treatments* and *scriptments*. All are rough sequential tellings of a story, generally in present tense and in third-person. But treatments don't typically include a full pass of a scene's dialogue, whereas the unformatted draft does (as do many scriptments, and some series outlines as well). Because there's no one good industry term for this kind of document that has been adopted across both film and series, we'll call it an "unformatted draft" from here out.

Lots of writers write the earliest passes of their scenes in an unformatted way. They capture their thoughts on index cards, yellow notepads, any old word-processing software, you name it.

You may ask: why take this extra step? Why not simply write your first draft directly into the screenplay format?

Great question. It's not an extra step. It's writing. As we'll emphasize throughout the rest of the book, scenewriting is all about revision. Every revision brings you closer towards perfecting your scene. The more drafts you can get through the better, and this is simply the first.

In addition, an unformatted draft has great psychological importance. For many writers, even seasoned veterans, looking at their work in proper screenplay format can give it a false veneer of finality. A formatted scene *looks* done, even if it isn't, and that can make it harder to edit. An unformatted draft looks like the work-in-progress it actually is.

In short, the unformatted draft is valuable because it both encourages experimentation and invites subsequent revision.

Let's Get This Party Started

To start, you'll need to establish where your scene is set, the time of day, who is present, and what they are doing when the scene starts. There's no need to belabor it; this information can be delivered in a straightforward way through scene description, as in:

> West 10th and Bleeker at night. Carlos and Jess stand in the shadows waiting.

> The house. Noon. Aisha sits on her front porch still wearing her flannel pajamas and drinking her morning coffee.

> Several kids goof off on Prospect Street. The school bus is late.

> Aaron sweeps the floor of the empty library. He's falling asleep on his feet.

When and Where

What you write about the time of day and the locale should be only and exactly what your reader needs to keep them engaged with your story.

Everyone has experience with schools, doctor's offices, living rooms, athletic fields, streets, parking lots, grocery stores, and the like. If there is nothing about your location that makes it transcend the generic expectation of a familiar space, then you don't need to waste words on it. Same with the time of day. Noon is noon. Sunset is sunset. With this in mind, the following are all perfectly viable ways to set up a relatively familiar location and time[1]:

---

[1] These simple statements of place and time will evolve into *sluglines* in Chapter 8.

The lunch room, Crockett High School. Day.

The megamall parking lot. Morning.

Dr. Howard's pediatrics office. Lunchtime.

Here are a few examples of writers describing locations:

Michael Arndt quickly paints the picture of a pretty sad classroom on page 1 of LITTLE MISS SUNSHINE:

> RICHARD (45) stands at the front of a generic community college classroom—cinderblock walls, industrial carpeting.

On page 6 of MOONLIGHT, Jenkins offers a brief introduction to Juan's home:

> A plot of land, a modest bungalow set way back from the road, the longest grass driveway.

On page 14 of PARASITE, writers Bong Joon Ho and Han Jin Won describe Ki-Woo's first steps inside the mansion:

> Ki-Woo carefully follows Mun-Kwang inside. Indeed, the interior is stunning. But not excessive. The furniture and decorations are all tasteful.

In each case, the writers provide a few embellishing details—the "longest grass driveway," the "stunning" interior—but otherwise offer the barest essentials so that they can get on with the characters' story. These terse descriptions of locations might leave you wondering: but what about all my research? Was that all a waste of time?

Not at all. Brevity in describing a location is important to keep the story moving and your research informs more than just these introductory descriptions. Location research helps you imagine how your characters move through a space, what sounds and sights and objects impact their experience, what may preoccupy them in the location. In other words, your research will lend authenticity to your New York pizza joint scene. Even if it doesn't show up in the first line of location description, your research will distinguish your pizzeria from a coffee shop, library, spaceship, daycare center, or big box store as the scene progresses.

But there can be story reasons for scenewriters to add further details to a location. Consider Sal's Pizzeria in DO THE RIGHT THING. It's your typical New York pizza joint, except that on page 14 writer Spike Lee explicitly calls out the photos of famous white Italian-Americans that Sal has hung on the wall:

> All around Buggin' Out, peering down from the WALL OF FAME, are signed, framed, eight by ten glossies of famous Italian Americans. WE SEE Joe DiMaggio, Rocky Marciano, Perry Como, Frank Sinatra, Luciano Pavarotti, Liza Minnelli, Governor Mario Cuomo, Al Pacino and, of course, how can we forget Sylvester Stallone as Rocky Balboa: THE ITALIAN STALLION, also RAMBO.

Lee offers these extra details because they serve a specific narrative purpose: it's the exclusion of people of color in the photos (in a pizza joint that is almost exclusively supported by people of color) that ticks off Buggin' Out later in the scene.

Knock Knock . . .

Every time a new character appears in a scene, you must decide how much or how little you should write about that character. There is so much one can write about a person; how do you choose? Do you mention their race? Their attire? Their stature? Their age rage? Their hair and eye color?

Again, we encourage you to direct the reader's attention to what is essential for your story. If a character's race is important for story reasons, obviously you should include a clear description. Keep in mind, however, that leaving something out means that you're leaving it to your reader's imagination.

In an entertainment industry that is disproportionately white, male, straight, non-disabled, and cis-gendered, it is likely that your characters will be seen as white, male, straight, non-disabled, and cis-gendered if you don't write them otherwise. To combat this bias, you should actively and explicitly diversify your characters. Using names like Marquez, Gbeho, Nguyen, and Tanaka is one way to gently steer your readers and casting agents away from assumed whiteness and towards diverse ethnicities. A stronger approach is to draw from the awesome diversity that exists in our world. Explicitly identify non-male and non-cis characters, include people with disabilities, people of color, and people from different places of origin. It will take some research, but it's worth the effort.

Let's examine a few examples of character introductions to see what is—and isn't—called out.

On the first page of CAN YOU EVER FORGIVE ME?, writers Nicole Holofcener and Jeff Whitty introduce their protagonist as follows:

> Across the room, a well-worn cat tree sits in the corner, piles of New Yorkers, and LEE ISRAEL, around 50 and not trying very hard, is asleep in her clothes on the couch.

Here we get Lee's rough age and her general life attitude, the latter bit beautifully and efficiently realized by her sleeping in her clothing. But many of her characteristics (such as her race, height, weight, and attire) are left to the reader's imagination.

Barry Jenkins introduces Juan on page 1 of MOONLIGHT by detailing only his age range and his curiously mixed racial composition:

> At the wheel find JUAN (30's, some sort of Afro-Latino thing about him) pulling towards us and coming to a stop.

On page 1 of JOJO RABBIT, Waititi gives us the first glimpses of Jojo's imaginary best friend with a touch of mystery:

> A STRANGE FIGURE passes behind him, an ADULT, dressed in a NAZI UNIFORM. It feels ghostly and fantastical.

Here the reader is explicitly shown only snippets of information to pique curiosity. The missing details, other than his adult status, gender, and Nazi attire, are deliberately absent.

On page 1 of QUEEN & SLIM we are introduced to the film's two central characters.

> Our focus is directed toward a BLACK MAN and a BLACK WOMAN sitting in a small booth in the back.
>
> The MAN: has a slender frame and a laid back demeanor. He's not a fan of rocking the boat or ruffling feathers, but he ain't no punk either. For the purpose of this story we'll call him SLIM.
>
> The WOMAN: She's regal as fuck. She's not an easy laugh and she's always waiting for the other shoe to drop. For the purposes of this story, we'll call her QUEEN.

Waithe takes her time over the descriptions. That the characters are Black is essential to the story. She also spends some time contrasting their personalities.

At the start of LADY BIRD, Gerwig offers names and ages, impressively channeling the voice and attitude of the film's teen protagonist in her apathetic handling of Marion's age:

> Two women sleep together in a bed. Christine, aka Lady Bird, 17 years old. Her Mom, Marion, the age of Lady Bird's Mom.

Each of the descriptions above is brief and functional, but notice, too, how they're fun to read. They sum up their characters quickly and do so with a strong nod to their stories' tones.

Better Late Than Boring

Scenes get moving once readers know where they're taking place, who is there, and what those characters are doing. But given all the activities that you imagine happening in your scene, where is the right place to drop the reader in?

Consider the following:

> Fans fill the stadium while players stretch and throw around. A pitcher warms up off the mound. The National Anthem plays.

The setting is clear—we're at a baseball game—but there are no obstacles, no conflict. The actions described all deliver the same piece of information: that we're witnessing the preamble to a game. If the excitement of our scene takes place at some moment later in the game, there's no reason to start this early.

Fastforwarding, here's a new start:

> The pitch zips in . . .
>
> UMPIRE: Stee-rike!
>
> . . . and the radar gun flashes 103mph.
>
> Lyle steps out of the batter's box, dazed. The crowd is on its feet. The bases are loaded. The scoreboard reads 3–0 with two outs in the bottom of the 9th. He flexes his bruised right hand, trying to shake off the pain.

This scene begins *in medias res*, aka in the middle of actions already in progress. It drops the reader right into the confrontation between Lyle and the pitcher and engages them in a treasure hunt (see the previous chapter) to figure out what is going on.

Dropping the reader into the middle of your scene's chronology forces them to play an exciting game of catch-up. There's rarely a good reason to provide a meandering run-up to the action. Look back at the four examples that opened this section; they each began *in medias res* as well, instantly building in that important reader engagement with compelling questions: Who are Carlos and Jess waiting for in the shadows? Why is Aisha still in her pajamas at noon? What happened to the school bus? Why is Aaron so tired?

The second scene of MOONLIGHT offers a pulse-pounding introduction of the main character, Little:

> Three young boys (adolescents, 12/13 years old) with sticks chasing Little (similarly aged but smaller, a runt) who is running, terrified.
>
> The three boys laughing as they give chase but. . . this is not a game, more like a hunt.

When we first see him, Little is literally running for his life. Readers don't need to know what started the pursuit to be immediately engaged. What matters is answering the question: will Little escape or not?

On page 2 of the pilot script for DIRK GENTLY, writer Max Landis drops us right into a run-in between Todd and his landlord:

> The Ridgely is a smallish four story apartment building on fringes of San Diego, ancient and more than a little dilapidated.
>
> Todd rushes out, still in his boxers, to see DORIAN, 30s, dangerous looking white trash covered in tattoos, attacking his 1999 Honda Civic with a hammer.
>
> TODD: Dorian! Dorian stop, stop stop—
>
> DORIAN: Where's my money!?

No word of explanation is needed to preface the destruction of Todd's car, the reader is already hooked.

A scene from THE WAY WAY BACK (page 36) opens with Duncan sitting at the waterpark, as he apparently has been all day:

> Duncan is back on the edge of the same PICNIC TABLE, still sporting the jeans and T-shirt look.
>
> OWEN: I'm afraid I'm going to have to ask you to leave.
>
> Duncan looks back over his shoulder.
>
> DUNCAN: . . . What?
>
> OWEN: Yeah, you're going to have to take off. I'm getting complaints. You're having too much fun. It's making everyone uncomfortable.

Writers Faxon and Rash omit Duncan's entire day of sitting, choosing instead to start the scene at the end of the afternoon when Owen asks him to leave. Poor

Duncan can't seem to find a comfortable place anywhere, and cutting right to Owen's interruption continues this trend.

EXERCISE: Writing the Beginning

This exercise is about finding the optimal starting point for your scene.

The first step is to identify the central conflict, then make a list of the minimal background information needed to get the reader to it. Include the location, time of day, character(s), and whatever they're doing from just before the scene starts to when we first see them.

Now it's time to drop the reader right into your scene *in medias res*. You can start with an image, an action, or with a line of dialogue, but in any case begin as late as you can while still allowing your reader to make sense of what is happening (and to receive the important information about the story that the scene needs to deliver). Don't forget that you can offer them clues to get them engaged. Think back to Giannis from Chapter 6 and the treasure hunt that established him as a busboy at the Athena Diner.

Scenis Morghulis: All Scenes Must End

Next, jump to the end of your scene. This might seem a little weird, but figuring out how your scene ends gives you a beacon to follow when you're writing the middle. It's okay if what you do here diverges from what you planned in Part I. Note that skipping to the end like this isn't a technique that works for everyone, but if you're a first-time scenewriter we encourage you to give it a shot, even if only to rule it out later.

There are two important functions of scene endings. The first is that they have to *reveal* something new to your reader. The second is that they need to compel the reader to keep reading. These often happen in tandem.

Reveals

A *reveal* at the end of your scene is a new piece of information that refines, enhances, reverses, or otherwise expands your readers' understanding of the main character's journey. The subject of that reveal is often the point of your scene. If, for example, this is the scene in which the main character's missing dog is found, that is the reveal.

The newly revealed information could be the answer to one of these questions: What new thing does your character want? Why are they pursuing that goal? Is there a new obstacle in their way? What approach are they going to try, and what do they learn if they succeed or fail in that pursuit?

Some of this new information can filter in throughout the scene, but the ending often provides the most impactful reveal of new information for the reader.

Though by no means exhaustive, here are a few common types of reveals that you can consider for the end of your scene.

The Natural Ending

As discussed throughout Part I, many scenes consist of a character pursuing a specific scene goal. The natural ending in this case occurs when the scene goal is resolved, either up or down. Did they succeed or fail?

In the case of Todd and his landlord, Todd fails to keep Dorian from destroying his car:

> DORIAN: Get my money. Six hundred—
>
> TODD: But—
>
> DORIAN: I don't care. Call the cops. Nope. You won't. Cause I got you, don't I? I got you.
>
> Dorian, happy with his destruction, heads back to his house, a dingy little shit-hole house, directly next to The Ridgely. Todd stands staring at his beaten up car.

His car is pulverized, he still owes Dorian money, and he's standing outside in his underwear. But at least it's not raining.

The Cyclical Ending

A *cyclical ending* is one in which the scene ending refers back to its beginning. In dialogue it is known as a *call back* when a specific line is reiterated from earlier in the scene, but it can also be done with a recurrent action, sound, or a matched camera shot. In any case, a cyclical scene recalls its start, signaling to the reader that the scene is at a close by returning to where it began.

The first scene of THE WAY WAY BACK begins with Duncan removing his headphones because Trent demands his attention. The scene ends when Duncan has finally had enough of Trent and he puts his headphones back in, even though Trent is still talking:

> TRENT: So, what do you say? Let's try to improve that score. Aim higher than a three?
>
> Duncan sits back down, facing out the back. Grabs his iPod.
>
> TRENT: That sound good? You up for that, buddy?
>
> He puts his earphones in, as we. . . <u>BEGIN MAIN TITLES</u>

Duncan is listening to music in the car. That's not unusual for a teenager. But after Trent digs into him, Duncan goes back to his headphones. This return to where he began the scene signals to the reader that Duncan wasn't just listening to music, he was insulating himself from his horrible new father figure Trent—as he's clearly done before. Cyclical endings imply a recurrent pattern.

The Reversal Ending

In a *reversal ending* the scene concludes with a surprise piece of information that undermines the audience's expectations of what had been happening to that point.

The first scene of BOOKSMART is a whirlwind tour of Molly's bedroom. The reader is shown Molly meditating to a recording, while books, photos, and clothing around her room reveal her to be both the high school valedictorian and a devout feminist. The ending of this angelic picture comes as a jolt:

> MOTIVATIONAL VOICE: Stand upon the mountain of your success and look down at everyone who's ever doubted you. Fuck those losers. Fuck them in their stupid, fucking faces.

> Molly's eyes pop open. She removes her biteguard.

Guess there's a side of her we didn't know about.

The Unexplained Mystery Ending

Some scenes end with a mysterious or discordant turn that is more surprise than misdirection. These types of endings generally leave readers with an, "oh THIS is the type of world we're in" feeling.

In a scene from GET OUT (pages 26–30), Chris, Rose, and Rose's parents Missy and Dean talk over iced teas served by the family maid Georgina. That is until:

> Georgina has been pouring Chris' drink too long and his glass has overflown.

> MISSY: Georgina!

> Georgina snaps out of her daze. She realizes what she's done and starts to clean.

> MISSY: It's fine George, I'll get it. Maybe you need a nap.

> Georgina nods, smiles and walks away. Chris and Rose look at Dean. That was odd. Dean shrugs.

Georgina's silent catatonia is unexpected and goes unexplained, for now. Her action presents a disturbing counterpoint to the hosts' conversation about the party they are planning the next day, one that will make sense in hindsight but at this point creates mystery.

Inviting the Reader into the Next Scene

In addition to revealing new information to your reader, your scene should also end in a way that inspires further interest. Leave a well-loved character hanging off a cliff, for example, and it'll be hard for readers to put the script down.

Let's say your character achieves their scene goal. Success is great, but it can kill the momentum of your story if they no longer have anything they want to pursue. So it's good to remind the reader of your character's overarching goal to keep the story moving:

Betty gets past the bouncer, but her purse isn't where she left it. Where is it?

Kara gets to dance with Janelle but the song ends. Now what?

Detective Shovel discovers a bloody thumbprint. Whose is it?

If it's a down ending, what lesson did your character learn? Are they going to abandon their scene goal and live with the consequences, or will they try to come at it from another angle?

Betty can't get past the bouncer and is too angry to wait in line. How will she get home in the middle of the night with no money?

The band stops playing before Kara musters up the courage to ask Janelle to dance. Will she find another excuse to talk to her crush?

Detective Shovel strikes out at the crime scene. What's he gonna say to the Chief?

No matter what happens with your character's scene goal, the ending is a great place to remind your reader that the story must go on.

Back to the opening scene of LADY BIRD, Marion and Lady Bird are fighting while driving in their car. The conflict peaks when Marion refuses to use Lady Bird's chosen name:

LADY BIRD: CALL ME LADY BIRD LIKE YOU SAID YOU WOULD!

MARION: You should just go to City College, with your work ethic. City College and then to jail then back to City College. Maybe you'd learn how to pull yourself up and not expect everyone to do everything for you. . .

> They slow for a stop light and Lady Bird dramatically opens the
> door and rolls out of the car. Marion screams.

When Lady Bird throws herself from the car it impresses upon the reader just how impassioned, determined, and impetuous she can be. By ending the scene in that instant, readers are also left wondering what happened to her. Is Lady Bird okay? This question invites readers into the next scene.

The opening scene of BOOKSMART ends with the reveal that Molly approaches high school like a battle with necessary casualties along the way. This new information acts as an invitation too: what must her high school life be like in order to merit this approach? Readers will want to see what she's been up against, and witness this badass high schooler in action.

Near the end of EIGHTH GRADE, writer Bo Burnham chronicles Kayla's first friend-date with Gabe. The scene ends (page 100) in the middle of Gabe's impromptu magic show:

> And as Gabe struggles through his act, messing up here,
> dropping a prop there, Kayla watches him.
>
> Someone is doing something for her. And she is watching it.
>
> Smiling.
>
> Her world upside-down.
>
> The pressure, finally, for a moment, off.

For a girl who has struggled to be herself and to be accepted throughout the entire story, the ending of this scene invites the reader to see a future where Kayla can be herself and be okay.

We're Closing Early

When we looked at where to begin your scene, we encouraged you to start late in order to get to the good stuff. The same principle applies to endings: get out as quickly as you can in order to maintain your story's momentum.

Imagine a patient is in cardiac arrest at a hospital. Our main character, an ER doc, is trying everything to save him. But the patient dies. Do you need to show the flatlined EKG or have the doctor say "Time of death, 4:03pm"? If not, imagine ending the scene while the doc is still doing chest compressions. Cut to the next scene, where the doctor mourns the loss of her patient over a pint, exhausted and alone. Here we left the ER in the midst of the exciting action and explained the result of the doctor's efforts through her despondence later on.

Little's introduction at the start of MOONLIGHT features him locking himself in a condemned house while the bullies who were chasing him are outside.

> THE REAR BEDROOM: more light in here than in the front, from that window. Little edges up to it, leaned away to not be seen. Slowly, stealthily, he raises his eyes above the threshold, SEES the three little bad asses who chased him. On cue—
>
> THUMP! A ratty shoe clanging off the windowpane. Reflex— Little startles, throws himself against the adjacent wall.
>
> As he clinches his eyes closed, breath cloistered up in his chest—
>
> UP CUT TO:
>
> A GLASS PIPE
>
> . . . held up to catch the light.

The scene ends with the bullies throwing a shoe at the window. Little closes his eyes and holds his breath. He's safe, but nowhere near calm. Instead of showing the minutes—hours?—between this final scare and the time when Little feels safe enough to explore the house he's entered, Jenkins choses to cut from fear to exploration.

After Molly and Amy confront Pat the pizza guy in BOOKSMART (page 64), Molly cautiously asks him for a ride:

> MOLLY: Since we're already in the car, could you maybe. . .drive us there?

PAT: Sure, buckle up.

The girls start to buckle their seatbelts.

PAT: I WAS BEING SARCASTIC GET THE FUCK OUT OF
MY CAR.

We don't see them actually getting out of the car, feeling ashamed, and wondering what to do next. The scene ends here. All that other stuff that would follow is so logical that it need not be articulated.

In the scene where Lady Bird throws herself from her mother's car, we don't see her rolling on the asphalt, her mom pulling over, traffic stopping, and the ambulance arriving. The leap out of the car is the climax of the scene and the perfect place to exit it. The image that opens the next scene, of Lady Bird in a cast at school, tells the reader everything they need to know about what happened.

EXERCISE: Writing the End

To write your scene's ending, start by figuring out a satisfying reveal. What is the scene building to? It might be the resolution—or the necessary postponement—of the scene's driving conflict. It might be a new piece of information that shifts the reader's understanding of your characters, their goals, or their situations. What is the major point of this scene? What piece of information about the character's goal, motivation, obstacles, or approach are you revealing?

How do you want to present this new information to your reader? In other words, what signals the end of the scene? Is there a scenic goal that gets concluded? Is there a reversal, cyclical ending, or unexplained mystery?

What are you doing to invite your reader into the next scene? What is the narrative question you've constructed that they'll want to have answered?

What is the earliest point you can exit the scene? Can you satisfactorily end in the middle of an ongoing action?

When you've answered these questions for yourself, take a stab at writing the ending.

In the Middle with You

All that's left now is to construct the bridge that links the beginning and the ending of your scene.

In Chapter 3 you worked out at least one approach that your character attempts to overcome the obstacle they face. But you may not have gotten beyond broad-stroke descriptions of these attempts like "they beg" or "they lie" or "they threaten." To write the middle of your scene you'll need to flesh out the details of those ideas in scene description and dialogue.

Suppose you're writing the scene with Betty and you've decided that she will attempt to charm the bouncer into letting her back inside the club. Of course "charm" can mean all kinds of things to all kinds of people. What is the specific version of charm that *your* Betty comes up with in this situation? Is she demure or brash? Conniving or just plain funny?

Remember: character is revealed through action. What your character values and believes will be communicated through the choices they make. In other words, your character's actions and reactions will provide an understanding of who they are.

But showing your characters acting is not your only task. As mentioned in the previous chapter, you also have to engage the reader in these actions and how they are presented. Tools like constructing a treasure hunt, undermining reader expectations, or setting up a collision are great for this.

Once you've determined what you feel is the best form of "charm" for Betty, then you have to figure out how to present the details of that choice in such a way that your reader has an engaging time decoding and understanding them.

Here's one approach to writing Betty's attempt to charm the bouncer:

Betty glances at the bouncer. He's small and round. He's fumbling with his headset.

Betty turns to her friend.

BETTY: Can I borrow your lipstick?

The friend digs into her purse.

FRIEND: Pastoral Sunset, or Dragon Girl?

Betty checks out the bouncer again. The wire from his headset is now clumsily wrapped around his head and chair.

BETTY: Dragon.

Betty deftly applies a bright red splash to her lips. She swooshes her hair and saunters up to the velvet rope.

BETTY: Love your shirt.

Betty never has to say what she's going to do. Instead, she makes a quick character read of her opponent and then she acts, leaving the reader to piece together her intentions.

How long did it take you to connect the dots and figure out that Betty is trying to charm him? Is there a particular line or juxtaposition of lines that gives it away for you? Or is it not until the very end?

Our goal was for the majority of readers to deduce Betty's intentions at or before the moment she compliments the bouncer's shirt. The hints in the treasure hunt are numerous and all in support of the same conclusion: she deliberately puts on some lipstick, fixes her hair, and "saunters" over to him before throwing out a compliment. Betty could have been even more explicit—"You are one sexy bouncer, pal"—but this treasure hunt makes it more engaging.

So, what's going to happen next?

One Thing Leads to Another (But and Therefore)

Trey Parker and Matt Stone, the creators of SOUTH PARK, have observed that their best episodes are those where the scenes are connected by the words "therefore" or "but."[2] Something happens, *therefore* another thing happens. *But* then this happens. And so on.

Therefore is the causal glue that holds stories together. A character wants something, *therefore* they act to achieve their goal. And actions, of course, generate reactions (thanks, Newton!). A thing happens, *therefore* some other thing follows. The optimistic idea that we can change our world through our actions is entirely based on the reality of *therefore*. If there wasn't a *therefore*, our actions would be pointless.

But implies the discovery of something that wasn't anticipated in advance and must now be dealt with. *But* represents an obstacle (or upended expectations, as per the previous chapter). *But* stands directly in opposition to *therefore*.

This same language can be helpful in understanding the causal flow of a single scene. We know Betty tries to charm the bouncer; then what? Here's an example of how *but* and *therefore* might be used to string together Betty's attempts to get around him:

> Betty splashes on lipstick and compliments the bouncer in order to get back into the club.
>
> **But** he tells her to get to the end of the line.
>
> **Therefore** she decides to confess the truth—she left her purse inside and really needs to get it back quickly or she'll miss her bus.
>
> **But** he explains that he was just yelled at by his boss for letting someone else cut the line, so as much as he'd like to help, he can't.
>
> **Therefore**, Betty . . .

Do you see how a chain of actions for an entire scene can easily emerge from these two words?

---

[2] MTVU Stand In, episode air date October 3, 2011.

Betty tries to charm the bouncer. It might work, it might not. Her action is going to lead to some reaction. Will it be a *therefore* or a *but*? Here are a few options, each of which takes the scene in an entirely different direction and opens up opportunities to test her further.

Option 1: ("*but* he's impervious to her charm.")

> BOUNCER: Back of the line.

Option 2: ("*but* he's not interested in women, so her charm is probably misguided.")

> BOUNCER: Thanks. My husband picked it out.

Option 3: ("*therefore* he gets creepy.")

> The bouncer ogles her.

> BOUNCER: Right back atcha, sexy.

The *buts* of options 1 and 2 will both force Betty to try a different approach. Option 3 is a "be carefully what you wish for" kind of response. Her charm seems to have worked, and she might be able to get this guy to let her back inside. But at what cost?

What's at Stake

The causal sequence of your characters' actions and reactions will push your story forward. But another thing will be happening as well: as your characters struggle towards their goals their stories will begin to embody the thematic content that you figured out back in Part I.

As a reminder, theme is the message you're delivering with your larger story, like: everyone grows up eventually; capitalism is destroying the planet; or, your lies always come back to haunt you.

When your characters push harder and raise their personal stakes, you have the opportunity to either punish them or reward them for their efforts. And that's where your thematic content is going to come into play.

Back to BOOKSMART, Amy and Molly scare Pat the pizza delivery guy and demand the address of the party. But Pat doesn't cave. Instead, he calls them reckless for jumping in a car with a strange man (him). He excoriates them for not having a weapon, only to reveal that he has his own gun. Yikes! The stakes are suddenly much higher for the girls. Pat continues calling out how their naiveté and stupidity could easily end up getting them assaulted or killed. Finally, shamed and cowed, Amy changes her approach. She politely asks Pat for the address, which is probably what they should have done all along. And he gives it to them.

In this scene, Molly and Amy do something extremely dangerous without even considering the danger they've put themselves in. Thematically, Molly and Amy's titular booksmarts have come at the cost of being world-smart. They might ace every lesson in class but in this scene they're schooled in the "real" world by a lowly pizza delivery guy. They need to eat a bit of humble pie in order to see themselves as the "normal" high school kids they are trying so hard to catch up with.

In THE WAY WAY BACK (page 59), Duncan's first real task at the water park is to take some cardboard away from a group of breakdancers. He tries to get their attention, but no one listens. So he turns off their music, making them all upset. He reaches for the cardboard, but one imposing dancer physically blocks him. The stakes are going up. The dancer makes Duncan dance in order to get their cardboard. So he does. It's clumsy and embarrassing. But the dancers embrace his earnest efforts and let him do his job, giving him the cardboard and dubbing him "Pop 'n Lock." By rewarding—rather than humiliating—Duncan for being his less-than-suave self, writers Faxon and Rash signal a path forward for this character struggling to find his way.

In JOJO RABBIT (page 29), Jojo has discovered Elsa secretly and illegally living in his sister's room. He knows that Elsa is there by his mother's invitation. So he waits for his mother to come home and begins testing whether or not she will confess to harboring Elsa. He mentions hearing his sister's ghost upstairs but she dismisses it as rodents. He subtextually calls Elsa a dirty rat—another test—and his mother reacts angrily but doesn't come clean. Her persistent lies raise the stakes—is Jojo losing his mother? Later he asks if she loves anyone else but she dodges the topic. He cannot reconcile how someone he loves so much could do something that he thinks is so wrong, but his mother's resistance is what sets him on the journey of questioning and rejecting his Nazi youth indoctrination.

EXERCISE: Filling out the Middle

You've written the beginning. You've written the end. To get from one to the other you can build causality, using *but* and *therefore* statements to advance the action.

Write down the first thing your character does ("Betty tries to charm the bouncer.") This action will trigger either a *but* or a *therefore*, which precipitates a new action until you reach your scene's conclusion. Map this out in shorthand until you know the sequence of causal events that comprise your scene. Be sure that the stakes are increasing with each attempt.

Paste the beginning and ending of your scene into the same document. Now, following your causal roadmap, write the scene description and dialogue to fill in the middle. Be sure to utilize the engagement strategies from Chapter 6 (treasure hunts, upended expectations, collisions/anticipation, and spectacle) to keep your reader involved!

8 Formatting for Fun and Profit

The unformatted draft you wrote in the previous chapter is a perfectly functional scene. It is an ordered sequence of events and actions that could be read aloud and understood as a story. But it isn't a script. Not yet. Because it's not in the proper screenplay format.

Screenplays are expected to look a certain way. It's important to learn and follow the screenplay format, because anyone reading your script will expect you to do so. Thankfully, there are plenty of software packages out there to manage the margins and fonts and other picky format-specific things that literally have nothing to do with your story. But there are other standards and conventions that are more than cosmetic. As you will see, these specialized elements and extensions of the screenplay format are valuable storytelling tools in and of themselves.

The truth is, there isn't one single "proper" way to format a screenplay. Anyone who claims to teach you otherwise is misinformed. One source may say that scene headings *must* be bold, another source will say that they are never bold. Some sources say scene heading elements must, without any question, be separated by commas, others say dashes, still others say periods. It's madness.

We see no value in joining that debate. The point is to tell a good story through your script and the formatting you use should support that aim. We will share what we feel are particularly effective formatting strategies, drawing from successful examples. Those examples might contradict each other, but hey, that's just further evidence that what is right for you is what *works in your script*.

If you find the lack of official precise guidelines off-putting, please remember two things. First, this means you are free to pick any screenplay "standard" that resonates with you and follow it without fear that you're somehow messing up horribly. And second, take comfort in the fact that your story is more important than draconian adherence to a single formatting standard. After all, you want to be evaluated for your skills as a storyteller, not as a measurer of margins.

Courier? I Don't Even Know Her!

Below are three examples of formatted screenplay pages. Page 60 from Greta Gerwig's LADY BIRD, page 64 from BOOKSMART by Halpern & Haskins, Fogel, and Silberman, and page 10 from Jordan Peele's GET OUT. All successfully produced screenplays, all similarly—but not identically—formatted.[1]

The first thing to point out is that the font is 12-point Courier. Courier is a fixed-width font and comes in a bunch of flavors like Courier New and Courier Prime. All are acceptable.

An aside: Does this mean you HAVE to use 12-point Courier? Our answer is the same for everything we cover in this chapter: you can eschew these standard operating practices if you want. But why would you? The goal is to remove as many obstacles as you can between your script and your reader. To go through the effort of writing a brilliant scene only to have someone throw it away because you used Comic Sans would be sad. Following conventions is a sign that you know what you're doing.

A second aside: conventions change. The best way to understand standard operating practice is to read current scripts and talk to other screenwriters. Stay informed about the latest standards and practices. We don't expect any radical shifts in a format that has held relatively constant for decades, but small changes happen all the time and they do add up. So watch for them and adopt them as needed.

Now back to the example pages:

The left margin on all three example pages is 1.5 inches, the right margin is 1 inch (ragged, not justified), the top is 1 inch, and the bottom varies but doesn't go smaller than 1 inch. All three examples have page numbers in the upper right.

---

[1] Note that from here on out in this book, all examples we share from scripts will be presented in their proper formatting.

INT. CHURCH. DAY.

All of Xavier and Immaculate Heart of Mary are assembled for
Ash Wednesday Mass.

Everyone gets ash on their forehead. Julie looks on enviously
as Lady Bird jokes around with Jenna and flirts with Kyle
from across the aisle.

The priest repeats the incantation every time he applies
ashes to the foreheads.

                    PRIEST
          Remember that you are dust and to
          dust you shall return... Remember
          that you are dust and to dust you
          shall return....

INT. FAMILY/COMPUTER/MIGUEL'S ROOM. DAY.

Lady Bird sits at the computer with a list of instructions in
front of her - Marion, Larry, Shelly and Miguel stand behind
her.

                    LADY BIRD
          It's a new system - you just enter
          your social security number and...

She is presses ENTER and is lead you to a website that lists
all the schools in the UC system she applied to with a "yes"
or a "no" beside them. They all say no except for...

                    LADY BIRD (CONT'D)
          DAVIS?!

                    MARION
               (relieved)
          Davis is good. Maybe you should
          have looked at it.

                    LADY BIRD
          It's only half an hour away! Less
          if you're driving fast!

                    LARRY
          I went to graduate school there.

                    SHELLY
          Lots of smart people go to Davis.

                    LADY BIRD
          I thought Berkeley had to accept
          me. You and Miguel went there.
          I'm a legacy.

ure 8.1 *LADY BIRD page 60.*

INT. PIZZA DELIVERY CAR - NIGHT

PAT, the LIDO'S DELIVERY GUY, gets in the front seat holding
two PIES. He's grumbling to himself--

                    PAT
          Two half-cheese, half-sausage
          pizzas are just one cheese and one
          sausage pizza you fucking *morons*--

Amy and Molly rise from the backseat like it's a carjacking.
They've <u>tied their hair into ponytails in front of their
faces, like a makeshift mask</u>.

          MOLLY   AMY
EVERYBODY STAY CALM!   DON'T MOVE!

Pat SCREAMS BLOODY MURDER.

                    PAT
          WHAT THE FUCK?! What the fuck?!
          What the fuck is this?!

                    MOLLY
          WE ASK THE QUESTIONS!

                    PAT
          Oh my God oh my God is this some
          kind of Manson family bullshit?

                    AMY
          No! No! Everything is gonna be just
          fine, you're just gonna give us the
          address where you delivered pizza
          earlier tonight!

A beat.

                    PAT
          I'm sorry, are you guys out of your
          fucking minds? How old are you?

                    MOLLY
              (lowest possible voice)
          Does not matter!

                    PAT
          Okay, that did not make you sound
          older. So you're basically children
          and you willingly got into a
          strange man's car. Do you even have
          a weapon?

                                        (CONTINUED)

Figure 8.2 *BOOKSMART page 64.*

INT. ROSE'S CAR - DAY

Rose hums. Chris, in the passengers seat, looks through his camera at the passing trees. He snaps a test shot.

                    CHRIS
          How long has it been?

                    ROSE
          10 months, so a year basically;
          longest I've ever been away.

Chris takes out another cigarette. Rose promptly grabs it and opens the window.

                    CHRIS
          Whoa... whoa!! Come on! I'm a
          grown man. If a man says he wants
          a cigarette, a man should be able
          too- -

She throws it out the window.

                    CHRIS (CONT'D)
          Okay, so that's like a dollar. You
          basically just throwin' dollars
          out the window.

                    ROSE
          You shouldn't have bought them.

                    CHRIS
          I didn't buy them. Rod... Shit.

                    ROSE
          What?

                    CHRIS
          I almost forgot Rod.

EXT. LAGUARDIA AIRPORT - OUTSIDE THE TERMINAL - DAY

ROD WILLIAMS, 26, African American, a stocky TSA agent smokes a cigarette. His cell phone rings.

                    ROD
          'Sup?

INTERCUT WITH:

There is room for approximately 55 lines per page, not including headers/footers.

All of this should be automagically handled by your screenwriting software of choice. If there's a little variation between one package's format and another's, don't lose sleep over it.

A Minute Per Page

One of the major benefits of working with consistent font and margin choices is that you can estimate the run-time of a produced script from its page count. Turns out the math is pretty easy: it's one minute per page.

There are exceptions, of course. Aaron Sorkin's dialogue-rich script for THE SOCIAL NETWORK is 163 pages with a running time of only 121 minutes. The script for ALL IS LOST by J. C. Chandor has no dialogue at all and finishes up at a neat 31 pages for a 107 minute film. But for the most part, an hour-long TV script will be around 60 pages long, and a feature film script will be in the 80- to 110-page range.

Even if you have a scene goal that can be achieved (or not) within a few minutes, your first formatted draft might come in longer than three pages at this stage. Don't worry about that yet—we'll look closely at your scene's length in Chapter 9.

EXERCISE: Pick Your Software and Import Your Unformatted Draft

If you don't already have a favorite, pick a screenwriting program that you want to work with. Download it, install it, open it up, create a new document, and get familiar with how it works. Type a few lines of scene description, then some character names and lines of dialogue. Figure out how to re-classify blocks of text by turning some scene description into dialogue and vice versa. Once you have the basics down, cut and paste the unformatted draft you wrote in the previous chapter into the program, and format it all as scene description (for now).

A NOTE FOR EXPERIENCED SCENEWRITERS: By following the exercises in this chapter you will transform your unformatted draft into a properly formatted scene. These exercises are designed for a scenewriter who has never worked with the screenplay format before, so they walk through formatting your scene element by element. Each exercise has you format a different kind of element, so you will take multiple passes over your scene if you follow the exercises as presented.

If you are already comfortable with formatting, you may wish to skip all but the exercises at the end.

A Slugline Says What?

The first line in all three of the sample pages is what we refer to as a *slugline* (or *scene heading*). These are special lines in the screenplay format that signal a change of location and/or time. A new slugline signals a change of setting, though not necessarily a change of scene. They are left-justified and appear in allcaps. Note they do not always have to appear at the top of a page. Indeed, the sample pages from LADY BIRD and GET OUT each feature multiple sluglines.

Sluglines begin with an abbreviation: INT. for interior, EXT. for exterior. If your scene takes place inside, it will be INT., whether it's a house, a car, or a submarine. If you plan on having the scene pass in and out of a space, you can write your slugline INT./EXT. so the reader will know what's coming, or you can insert the appropriate slugs when the action moves inside/outside.

Directly after the introductory abbreviation is where you identify the scene's location. It could be very specific like "FAMILY/COMPUTER/MIGUEL'S ROOM" or general, like "CHURCH."

Scene headings can specify a sub-location and/or a time of day. You may also identify a scene as taking place in FLASHBACK (aka in the past) just as if you might identify it at SUNSET or DAWN. Again, the idea here is to specify what is important for the reader to understand regarding where and when the scene takes place, and not to be too long-winded about it. Clarity is key.

Below are example scene headings drawn from the same three scripts to highlight how much variation there can be in formatting sluglines. If a particular style appeals to you, adopt it, but try to stay concise and be sure to remain consistent throughout your screenplay.

In LADY BIRD, writer Greta Gerwig uses periods to distinguish between slugline elements. Note how the two kitchens are referenced differently but both are clear.

```
INT. LADY BIRD'S KITCHEN. EARLY AFTERNOON.

[...]

INT. KITCHEN. KYLE'S HOUSE. DAY.

[...]

EXT. SACRAMENTO STREETS. LATE AFTERNOON.

[...]

INT./EXT. 1994 TOYOTA COROLLA. EARLY EVENING.

[...]
```

In GET OUT, Jordan Peele generally uses a dash to delineate elements, but also brings in a period and slash from time to time. Note how he distinguishes flashbacks from present day at the head of the slugline, and identifies a location that is seen on a television screen.

```
EXT. ARMITAGE ESTATE - AFTERNOON

[...]

FLASHBACK - INT. SMALL APARTMENT - NIGHT

[...]

PRESENT DAY - INT. MISSY'S OFFICE. NIGHT

[...]

INT. HOSPITAL ROOM - DAY (TELEVISION)

[...]
```

The following examples from BOOKSMART all use dashes to separate slugline elements. They also include a slightly different approach from the one used in LADY BIRD to identify a scene set inside and outside of a car.

```
EXT. LUNCH ROOM - CROCKETT HIGH SCHOOL - DAY

[...]

EXT. PICNIC TABLE - THE VALLEY - DUSK

[...]

EXT. MARINA/INT. JARED'S MUSCLE CAR - NIGHT

[...]

INT. LIVING ROOM - NICK'S AUNT'S HOUSE - NIGHT

[...]
```

EXERCISE: Writing Sluglines

Read through your unformatted scene from Chapter 7 and insert a slugline wherever you need to signal a change of setting and/or time. Many scenes are written with a single location and time, so you may only need one slugline at the very beginning of your scene. Format all of your sluglines in a consistent style, differentiating between location, sub-location, and time. Feel free to model your style on the examples in this section or from another script of your choosing, but keep it simple and consistent.

You Lookin' at Me?

Scene description was introduced as a storytelling tool in Chapter 5. Here we expand upon things you can (and are expected to) do in terms of formatting that will enhance and clarify scene description for your reader.

Callouts

One of the most effective ways to draw your reader's attention to a specific word or phrase is to write it in allcaps. Scenewriters allcap words to call attention to something that shouldn't be missed. This can be done when introducing a new character's name (SLIM), or highlighting a specific object (THE IDOL), message (ROSEBUD), sound (a GUNSHOT), or action (she JUMPS). Because of this, we call the entire class of these kinds of uses *callouts*.

Here are two examples of allcap callouts from page 87 of EIGHTH GRADE. One calls out an object, the other a written message:

```
Kayla and Dad are sitting next to each other on plastic lawn
chairs around a small fire burning in the patio's fire-pit.

Kayla looks down at the TIME CAPSULE in her lap.

Its writing glows by the light of the fire: TO THE COOLEST
GIRL IN THE WORLD.
```

This short block of scene description from page 132 of SCOTT PILGRIM VS. THE WORLD features multiple callouts of actions, sounds, objects, and characters as Scott wards off his attackers:

```
Kim drives a hardcore beat. Sex Bob-Omb ROCK THE FUCK OUT.
HIPSTERS ATTACK SCOTT PILGRIM to the BEAT. Scott swings his
FLAMING RED SWORD, exploding each attacker into COINS.
```

When used in dense blocks of scene description, allcap callouts will signal the most important information to the reader. A quick scan of the above block signals the band rocking and Scott fighting. The extra details are there for the close reader but even the skimmer will get the basic idea.

You can also use allcaps to make shot callouts. We're not talking about specific camera directions like "dolly slowly into a silhouetted close-up" but more general, and often blunter, ways to help the reader see what you want them to see.

When Lester accuses his daughter of turning into her mother on page 72 of AMERICAN BEAUTY, the daughter storms off and Ball directs the reader towards Lester with "ANGLE on":

```
ANGLE on Lester, and the immediate regret in his eyes.
```

A differently formatted use of this same technique appears on page 10 of CAN YOU EVER FORGIVE ME?, an extra line break drawing even more attention to the shift of perspective:

```
        Marjorie excuses herself.

        ANGLE ON

        The bar as Lee gratefully finds it.
```

On page 78 of MOONLIGHT, Jenkins shows us Black's underwear hanging to dry. He then uses a shot callout—this time a reverse angle—to let us see the same thing through Black's eyes:

```
        Dangling from a wire hanger, panning with the flow of an
        oscillating fan: the underwear we'd seen Black wear before,
        still damp in the humid air.

        REVERSE ANGLE: BLACK'S FACE, eyes fixed on the underwear,
        studying them with a mixture of shock and reverence.
```

There's a long debate about how much "directing" a screenwriter can get away with. The truth of the matter is, screenwriters are directing all the time. By describing one aspect of a particular setting and not a thousand others, the screenwriter is guiding the reader's attention to that detail and offering a future director a visual journey through the story. Sometimes a specific shot callout is just what you need, but it's generally more acceptable to guide the reader's attention where you want it without identifying camera directions.

Transition Callouts

Related to ANGLE ONs, CLOSE ONs, and REVERSE ANGLEs are periodic callouts of editorial actions you can fold into your scene. These aren't examples of scene description per se, but since we're talking about meta-level camera callouts, we'll take a minute to talk about transition options like FADE IN, CUT TO, and DISSOLVE TO.

Some scripts open with FADE IN, and usually the same ones end with FADE OUT. Neither are required to signal the beginning or end of a film, but they add a nostalgic grace to the transition in or out of the unique world of the film.

Between scenes you will sometimes see a right-justified transition like CUT TO: added by a screenwriter to call attention to the change of scene. This isn't officially necessary because a new slugline indicates that a cut is happening. Still, there are moments when you can get narrative mileage out of even this very basic transition like when you really need to underscore a quick cut between locations.

On page 4 of the pilot script for THE WIRE, writer David Simon fades out of the opening scene in such a way that highlights detective McArdle's take on the current state of his city:

```
MCARDLE turns around, takes in the scope of the tragedy that
is Baltimore. On our DETECTIVE, delighted with life,

                                                    FADE TO:
                        MAIN TITLES
```

On page 16 of JOJO RABBIT, Waititi ends a sequence from the injured Jojo's point of view with a fade, suggesting poor Jojo's fall from consciousness:

```
Adolf leans in, smiles and gives us the thumbs up. Jojo's
BLOODIED THUMB comes into view.

                                                    FADE OUT.

INT. HOSPITAL - WARD - DAY

- A woman's face comes in to focus. This is Jojo's mother,
ROSIE BETZLER. As she reaches the bed, she stops, puts her
hand over her mouth. Her eyes well with tears.
```

As a general rule, use these new formatting tools with care to avoid a script cluttered with so many callouts and transitions that they distract the reader from the important work of understanding your story. If everything is capitalized then nothing will get attention. Allcaps works because they provide a valuable CONTRAST to catch the reader's eye. IF YOU OVERDO IT, YOUR READER WON'T KNOW WHERE TO LOOK. SEE?

EXERCISE: Format That Scene Description

Take a pass through your entire scene, adding callouts and (if you're feeling them) transitions to your scene description. Remember that if this scene is the first time a character is introduced to the reader, put their name in allcaps, too.

You Got Something to Say?

As you can see from the example pages, dialogue is significantly indented. This makes it easy for your reader to tell when someone is talking. All three examples have the dialogue left-justified with approximately 2.5 inch margins. Character names have about a 3.5 inch margin and appear in allcaps.

In the example page from GET OUT, you may have noticed a strange "(CONT'D)" appearing once after Chris's name:

```
        Chris takes out another cigarette. Rose promptly grabs it and
        opens the window.

                        CHRIS
                Whoa... whoa!! Come on! I'm a
                grown man. If a man says he wants
                a cigarette, a man should be able
                to- -

        She throws it out the window.

                        CHRIS (CONT'D)
                Okay, so that's like a dollar. You
                basically just throwin' dollars
                out the window.
```

Not every writer uses (CONT'D) but it's there as a signal to the reader that despite the dialogue being interrupted by some scene description, it is still supposed to be one block of dialogue spoken by the same character. Most screenwriting software packages can automatically add (CONT'D)s if you decide you like using them.

Wrylies

The example pages from BOOKSMART and LADY BIRD feature parenthetical notes appearing left-justified at around 2.9 inches under character names, things like "(relieved)" and "(lowest possible voice)." These are known as *wrylies* or *parentheticals*.

Wrylies are powerful little tools that allow scenewriters to clarify something about how a block of dialogue is to be delivered. For example, consider the following sarcastic line:

```
                    BETTY
          I really appreciate how safe
          you're keeping all of us.
```

As written, this dialogue may be considered sincere. We could reword the line to clarify the tone, or use a wrylie to make it perfectly clear, such as:

```
                    BETTY
                (sarcastically)
          I really appreciate how safe
          you're keeping all of us.
```

In the example page from BOOKSMART, for example, Molly's wrylie—"lowest possible voice"—helps clarify Pat's next line of dialogue: "Okay, that did not make you sound older." Without the wrylie to clarify Molly's intonation, his response wouldn't make much sense.

Wrylies are unnecessary for most dialogue. They should be used only for clarification and not to micromanage your actors. After all, you're the expert on writing, they're the experts on acting. However, when a line of dialogue can have multiple meanings and needs some specific clarification, a wrylie can be the perfect solution.

Pauses and Interruptions

In addition to signaling particular inflections or clarifications, parentheticals can also act as a brief pause within dialogue, inject a small action, or clarify who is being addressed.

A conversation between Paula and Black on page 66 of MOONLIGHT uses parentheticals in four different ways:

```
                    PAULA
          Yeah it sound funny to me too. But
          I am your mother, ain't I? You can
          talk to me if you want to.
          Or at least somebody, you got to
          trust somebody, you hear?
               (then)
          You talk to Teresa?

                    BLACK
          Yeah.

                    PAULA
          How she doing?

                    BLACK
               (Shrugs)
          Good.

     Paula mimics Black's shrug...

                    PAULA
          "Good."

     ...face curling into a beautiful, teasing smile. Hard to not
     love this woman, hard to not give her infinite second
     chances.

                    BLACK
          When you go home?

                    PAULA
          Home?
               (beat)
          This is home. I mean... they
          'lowin' me to stay and work as
          long as I like. I figured, you
          know, might as well help other
          folks, keep myself out of trouble.

                    BLACK
          That's good, mama.

                    PAULA
          Yeah... I think it is too.
               (a deep breath)
          I really do.
```

Jenkins uses both "(then)" and "(beat)" to inject a brief pause into the dialogue. Some writers also use (and) or (pause) for this purpose.

Both "(a deep breath)" and "(Shrugs)" work as a kind of shorthand. They allow the writer to sneak in a minor action without using an entire line of scene description. If you tried to accomplish either of these in scene description, you'd at least need to identify the subject of the action, such as:

```
Black shrugs.
```

Or:

```
Paula takes a deep breath.
```

These parenthetical shortcuts get you the same effect, but they use less space and are less disruptive than breaking into a full line of scene description.

MORE and CONT'D

A very format-specific use of a parenthetical is when a block of dialogue carries across a page break, which you indicate to the reader by using (MORE), as in this example from the bottom of page 16 of JOJO RABBIT:

```
                    JOJO
          Why so happy? Your son is ugly
          like a monster.

                    ROSIE
          You're no monster. You're still my
          beautiful Jojo.
               (MORE)

                                        (CONTINUED)
```

On the top of the next page, a (CONT'D) signals the continuation of Rosie's dialogue:

```
        CONTINUED:

                        ROSIE (CONT'D)
                  Besides the doctors are confident
                  those scars will heal and you'll
                  get most of the movement back in
                  your leg. But I'm just happy to
                  have you back home.
```

Note this particular script also has (CONTINUED) at the bottom of the page and CONTINUED: at the top of the next to identify that the scene itself also continues over the page break. These types of auto-generated indicators are usually handled by your screenwriting software of choice, but it is still useful to be aware of the conventions and their meanings.

Trailing Off, Interrupting, and Talking Over

At first glance, the linear sequencing of dialogue in the screenplay format suggests that conversations must occur with one person speaking to completion, then another person speaking to completion, and so on. Of course, real conversations don't always work that way. People pause, stutter, interrupt each other and talk simultaneously. Thankfully, all of this stuff is possible within the format, as we began to see in Chapter 5 but will expand upon here.

Consider page 19 from EIGHTH GRADE, which captures the horribly and wonderfully awkward dinner conversation between Kayla and her dad. Burnham skillfully accentuates their dynamic in dialogue by infusing it with pauses and interruptions throughout:

Formatting for Fun and Profit

```
                    KAYLA
          Fine. What.

                    DAD
          Okay...But you gotta listen. Don't
          be angry before I even say it or
          you won't really hear it, okay?

                    KAYLA
          OHMYGOD, Dad, just say it--

                    DAD
          Alrightalrightokay -- I'm saying
          it....

Dad gathers himself. Pauses.

                    KAYLA
          DAD.

                    DAD
          I'm THINKING.

Kayla closes her eyes. So frustrated.

                    DAD (CONT'D)
          ...I...I think you're so cool-

                    KAYLA
              (huge huff, so embarrassed)
          Dad, seriously, I'm gonna stop
          eating with you if--

                    DAD
          You said I could say my one thing
          so let me say it...

                    KAYLA
          ....

                    DAD
          I think you're so cool. When I was
          your age, I wasn't cool like you.
          You have all these interests and
          you make all your videos and stuff
          and that's so great and cool.
          But...You know but sometimes I
          just worry that you don't put
          yourself out there--

                    KAYLA
          Please stop--
```

Note Burnham's use of pauses and interruptions everywhere—Dad even interrupts himself! And what do you make of the line where Kayla has no dialogue at all? Note, too, the key allcap callouts that provide emphasis in the dialogue just like they do in scene description. Some scenewriters use *italics*, underlines, or **bold text** for this kind of emphasis as well.

Kayla and Dad take turns speaking in this scene even though they frequently interrupt each other. However, if you would like two characters to speak simultaneously, format their lines side-by-side, as the above example page from BOOKSMART:

```
Amy and Molly rise from the backseat like it's a carjacking.
They've tied their hair into ponytails in front of their faces,
like a makeshift mask.

          MOLLY                           AMY
EVERYBODY STAY CALM!             DON'T MOVE!

Pat SCREAMS BLOODY MURDER.
```

This *dual dialogue* signals that two characters are speaking at the same time. However, it is also difficult to read (and listen to), especially if the dialogue is full of interruptions and parentheticals as well.

Whatever screenwriting software you choose should be able to format dual dialogue, but for clarity's sake, use with caution.

Other Ways Characters Can Talk: O.S. and V.O.

Most dialogue occurs between characters who appear *on-screen*. What this means is that in a filmed version of your scene, the audience would be able to see the characters as they speak. Unless otherwise noted, it is assumed that all dialogue in a screenplay occurs on-screen.

When dialogue is identified as *off-screen* (by using the letters O.S., or sometimes referred to as *off-camera* with the letters O.C.), it means we can hear a character speaking from outside the camera's view. For example, imagine Betty talking on the phone with her friend. We can hear the friend's voice but we don't see her.

```
                    FRIEND (O.S.)
               You left your purse inside the
               club?

                    BETTY
               Yeah, sorry, I'm going to be late.
```

Yet another way to have a character speak would be to use voiceover (V.O.). V.O. differs from O.S. because it is used to show an on-screen speaker narrating their internal thoughts or an off-screen narrator talking to the audience. If Betty is reliving the purse scene in her own memory, for example, you might see V.O. used as follows:

```
                    BETTY (V.O.)
               I'll never forget that night...
```

Or, if there is an omniscient third-person narrator:

```
                    NARRATOR (V.O.)
               Betty freaked out when she
               realized she no longer had her
               purse.
```

Be advised that speaking directly to the reader in V.O. transforms your scene from one that's simply *unfolding* in front of the reader to one that's being *told* to them. This stylistic choice isn't for everyone, but it might be just the thing if you want to bring a prose-like, meta-level awareness to your scene.

Here is an example from page 36 of EIGHTH GRADE, where the reader hears the narration from one of Kayla's self-help videos in V.O. during Kennedy's birthday party.

```
        Kayla enters the family room. Stops in the doorway.

                            KAYLA (V.O.)
                   Okay, so, like, "Putting Yourself
                   Out There". What does that mean?
                   Like, Putting Yourself Out There?
                   Where's There? Okay, these are all
                   good questions but they're also
                   bad questions.

        Kayla inches towards the couch, stands behind it, forces a
        smile.
```

EXERCISE: *Format Your Dialogue*

Go over your scene and format all of your dialogue. As with your scene description, a lot of it should transcribe directly from your unformatted draft. But take the time to handle any pauses, interruptions, wrylies, O.S. and V.O. identifications properly. And then celebrate—you have written your first fully formatted draft of your scene!

PART III

Perfecting

Welcome to Part III, where you'll take that first draft of your scene and *perfect* it.

"But," you say, "I just did everything I could to make my scene as good as it could be!"

A perfectly reasonable response. At first glance, revision sounds a lot like: *do everything you just did, only better.* That's a tough ask.

Don't worry. We have no plans to return you to the fray unprepared. This third and final part is dedicated to guiding you through the critical revision process with the support it deserves. You'll soon see that there's plenty you can do to upgrade your first draft, and it starts by looking at your work in a slightly different way.

As strange as it might sound, one of the hardest parts of rewriting is understanding what you've actually written instead of what you thought you wrote. The attic is supposed to seem really spooky, but is it coming off as quaint and rustic? You've tried to ratchet up the tension as Kara approaches Janelle, but does it play out as dragging and dull?

Whether your scene is too long, your characters speak "on the nose," or your exposition is too obvious, perfecting will get you to the well-paced, engaging, and meaningful scene that you imagined when you started. Each of the following chapters will introduce new ways to *analyze* what you've got on the page and help you objectively understand how it works (or doesn't). Informed by your discoveries, you will be able to *revise* accordingly, and realize everything in your scene that you set out to achieve.

Perfecting is not always a linear process: give yourself space to experiment, explore, invent. Some paths will lead forward, others back, but you will get there eventually. Revision will transform even a functional story into something magical. Perfecting will show you how.

9 Check Your Length

The length of your scene matters. A lot. Why?

For starters, everyone's busy. Getting anyone to read your script is tough and if you hand them a tome to leaf through, it's even tougher. Furthermore, if you're lucky enough to have your script go into production, every page translates into higher cost. So it's important to make every line of dialogue and scene description worth the effort.

Overwritten scenes spell out too much for the reader, repeat information, and take too much time over moments that could be concise and pithy. Every scene needs to engage from the jump and keep engaging.

You might conclude from these observations that shorter is always better. As a general rule, that makes sense: if you can deliver the same reading experience in fewer pages, why not go with the shorter version? The scene should only run as long as it needs to do its work without irrelevant details, actions or dialogue.

There is such a thing, however, as *underwriting*. If you leave too much out, readers can become confused about what's happening, lose track of a character's motivation, or miss a critical story point. Too little information is as bad as too much: readers will lose faith in your writing, close your script, and get on with their lives.

The goal of this chapter is to help you find your scene's perfect length: long enough to accomplish all the necessary story work, but concise enough to grab and hold your reader's attention.

The Bare Necessities

Every line of scene description and dialogue in your scene counts. The best ones further your story in an engaging and informative way. They are doing the important and necessary work they should be doing, moving your scene forward plot-wise, thematically, and tonally with each word. Any lines that aren't contributing to this forward momentum are not just falling short, they're actively bringing your scene down. There is really no such thing as a "neutral" line. Lines either strengthen your script or they are wasting space, time, and money.

A scene is overwritten when it contains material that doesn't further your story. This means it is possible for a one-page scene to be overwritten, just like it's possible for a five-page scene to be overwritten. It all depends on how much story information the scene is designed to convey.

As mentioned earlier, most scenes in most scripts run from two to four pages. Scenes of this length are the structural units from which larger stories are assembled. If you are a seasoned scenewriter, you know this well. If you are new to the process, you may find this surprising, especially if you're looking at a six-page first draft. But there's a very good chance that your six-page draft is actually a two-page scene in disguise.

The key to assessing your scene's length is to read it carefully for the story content it provides. Those moments that are integral to the story should stay: your character, their goal, the obstacles, basically everything we covered in Part I. Stuff that isn't necessary should go—even if it's brilliant on a word-by-word level.

You planned out your scene in Part I and executed that plan in Part II. Even if you followed your plan to the letter, the specifics of how your scene unfolds on the page are new. You have codified your plan in dialogue and scene description. This evolution is excellent and to be expected, of course. It's the writing process. But now it's time to evaluate whether everything you wrote was necessary. Odds are, your scene can be tightened up.

Below is a sample from Betty's story. It's a first draft cooked up to illustrate the important process of closely reading your script in order to revise it. Let's evaluate what story work is being done in this example, with an eye towards culling everything that's overwritten:

EXT. DANCE CLUB - MIAMI - NIGHT

This is the QUAKING PALM, a huge Miami dance club. It takes up
an entire city block. It's surrounded outside by fancy cars and
well-dressed patrons. Low BASS notes with a Latin flavor emerge
like THUNDER from the fortress-like building.

A line of impatient club-goers waiting to get in stretches
around the block.

The front of the line stops at a VELVET ROPE. A BOUNCER and a
massive SECURITY GUARD work the door. Four women are waved in--
they're the lucky ones.

As they enter, BETTY and her friend, CARMEN, exit. They're
sweaty and tired and happy to be outside again. They make their
way to the street.

                    CARMEN
          When did you learn to samba?

                    BETTY
          Thanks, but I was faking it.

                    CARMEN
          Well, you looked good.

                    BETTY
          You're sweet, but I got nothing
          compared to you.

Betty tries to hail a cab, only to realize something.

                    BETTY
          Damn. Be right back.

                    CARMEN
          What is it?

She walks back up to the bouncer.

                    BETTY
          Hey--excuse me?

The bouncer turns to her.

                    BETTY
          I left my purse inside. Can you
          let me run in and grab it so I can
          get home?

                    BOUNCER
          Back of the line.

On a first glance, this example appears to be written perfectly well line by line. However, when assessing a scene's length, it doesn't matter how well a line is written, what matters is whether or not that line is necessary for telling your story. In other words, in revising this example, we're not on the hunt for poorly written lines, we're looking to cut lines that aren't carrying their story weight, no matter how well-written they may be.

To determine what's necessary in the example, we start by identifying the core story elements from Part I. Betty (our character) is at a Miami dance club (setting). She wants to get home after a night of dancing (goal). But she forgot her purse inside the club and needs to get it back first (scene goal). She asks the bouncer (obstacle) to let her back inside (approach) but he doesn't comply. Now she must try something new (other approaches) or leave her purse behind.

The quest to retrieve her purse is what drives Betty's story forward. All lines furthering that story are necessary. The others are not.

Consider the opening two blocks of scene description. These lines identify the club's size, its name, and the fact that it's busy. They add flavor, but the only lines that are truly necessary to Betty's story are those that reinforce how hard it is to get inside the club (the obstacle). If she could walk right back in there would be no conflict, so describing the queue and the bouncer are essential.

Over-describing is one of the most common forms of overwriting, and that's exactly what's happening in this description of the club. How can you tell?

Great question. Try reading the scene while covering one sentence or block of scene description at a time and ask: Does the scene work without it? If so, then the sentence or block is overwritten and can be cut.

In the example, the setting is established in the slugline. As we've suggested, it's probably worth reinforcing the long line of patrons and the bouncer because of their relevance as obstacles, but other details about the club can be removed. What does it matter, for example, that the club takes up an entire city block?

Removing the extraneous details, we are left with:

```
EXT. DANCE CLUB - MIAMI - NIGHT

A line of impatient club-goers waiting to get in stretches
around the block.

BETTY and her friend, CARMEN, exit. They're sweaty and tired
and happy to be outside again. They make their way to the
street.
```

We've made cuts but what, if anything, has been lost? The club is certainly rendered with less detail. The unique specifics of the Quaking Palm might be interesting (and fun to write), but they digress from the story. We must remember to focus on a character in pursuit of a goal. That's what drives the story and will draw readers in. Cut unrelated details and the reader gets there faster.

The next section to consider is the dialogue between Betty and Carmen. Their exchange adds some detail to their experience in the club and their appreciation for one another, but if you cover up their exchange it's clear that Betty's line "Be right back" is the only one that relates to the core story. The rest is filler.

Irrelevant dialogue is another common type of overwriting. It can be fun to let your characters ramble, but our goal at this stage of revision is to keep only what's necessary.

Pruning the excess, we're left with:

```
        Betty tries to hail a cab, only to realize something.
                        BETTY
            Damn. Be right back.
```

After Betty's line, the rest of the scene is all necessary goal- and obstacle-establishing stuff. It may not be the most polished writing yet, but it directly pertains to the story, so we'll keep it.

The adjustments we've made to this scene cut its length nearly in half:

```
EXT. DANCE CLUB - MIAMI - NIGHT

A line of impatient club-goers waiting to get in stretches
around the block.

BETTY and her friend, CARMEN, exit. They're sweaty and tired
and happy to be outside again. They make their way to the
street.

Betty tries to hail a cab, only to realize something.

                    BETTY
          Damn. Be right back.

She walks back up to the bouncer.

                    BETTY
          Hey--excuse me?

The bouncer turns to her.

                    BETTY
          I left my purse inside. Can you
          let me run in and grab it so I can
          get home?

                    BOUNCER
          Back of the line, lady.
```

The amount of tone to fold back in at this point is a matter of taste and preference. If, for example, we wanted to bring details of the Quaking Palm back into the mix, we could revise the first part of the scene as follows:

```
EXT. THE QUAKING PALM - MIAMI - NIGHT

This is THE place to be. It's loud and busy with an endless
line stretching around the corner.

BETTY and CARMEN stumble out, exhausted.
```

EXERCISE: Throwin' Strikeouts

This exercise is about cutting your scene down to the bare necessities of the story. It's a chance to be bold and aggressive. You'll learn a lot about your story by trimming the fat, and you can always build things back up in a later draft if you overdo it.

Start with a printed copy of your scene and use a pen to mark it up. This can also be done digitally if you have the appropriate software. In either case, the salient point is that you're not directly changing the text of your scene in this exercise. That comes later.

Determine the necessity of each paragraph of scene description and dialogue by asking: Does my scene still work without it? To find out, cover one paragraph at a time and read what's left. If the scene still works then the paragraph isn't essential and you can ~~strike it out~~.

By doing this you may realize that the cabinet that you spent three paragraphs of scene description on doesn't actually play into the scene at all. ~~Goodbye, cabinet!~~ That page of chit chat that precedes the real conversational focus of the scene? It's a waste of space. ~~Adios, needless banter!~~

Now try the same trick with each line of your remaining (unstruck) paragraphs. Go line by line, cover one sentence at a time, and read around the covered portion. Does the paragraph still work? Does the dialogue accomplish what it needs to? If it does, then ~~you know what to do~~.

Remember: a line might be beautifully written. It might be poetry. It might make you all aglow with its grammatical completeness and complexity. That doesn't make it script-worthy. If it isn't germane to your story, circle it to show just how awesome it is. Then ~~strike it out~~.

Chapter 7 introduced the idea of starting your scene late and ending it early. Now is a great time to see if that's happening. See how much you can cut from the start of your scene before it no longer makes sense. Do the same with the ending. How late can you get into the action, and how early can you exit after it's resolved?

Once you've gone through your entire draft, ruthlessly striking through everything that isn't necessary, it's time to duplicate your scene file. Open up a new copy and actually delete the lines that you've struck out. Do so with confidence (after all, you're working with a copy of your scene, and you can always go back to the original draft if necessary).

The act of cutting will leave gaps that you'll have to fill in. For example, you may have to patch up conversations so they flow smoothly again, or re-introduce any objects, characters, or actions that play into the scene but were cut during the purge.

Once you've strung your scene back together, take a look at how much you were able to edit out. Does your scene's length more accurately reflect the amount of work it needs to do in your script? Might you need another pass? Reiterate the process if necessary, and keep bringing that page length down.

Whoa, I Think I Missed Something

The antithesis of overwriting is underwriting. Underwriting occurs when your scene fails to provide the story information that the reader needs to understand what's going on. You may think that your character's motivation is perfectly obvious, you may believe that you've dropped enough clues to make sense of a goal, or that a character's approach is entirely logical, but it doesn't always read that way to a first-time reader.

We're not talking about those moments where you are deliberately ambiguous. There will be times when you want to throw your reader something mysterious in order to engage their curiosity. Dropping clues is, after all, a core principle of the treasure hunt strategy we introduced in Chapter 6. There's mystery, however, and then there's confusion. The former leads the reader towards a logical conclusion; the latter is simply perplexing.

To demonstrate underwriting, let's say we're trying to establish that Kara is admiring her crush, Janelle, at the school dance. Here's a potential first draft of that scene description::

```
KARA looks over at a girl dancing by herself with pure joy.
```

Does this line do the work it is intended to do? Kara is introduced by name but Janelle is not; she's only referred to as "a girl." And there's no mention of Kara's crush. If this is all the information we provide about Janelle, readers won't understand who Janelle is or what Kara feels about her.

As the writers of Kara and Janelle's story, we are familiar with every detail. It makes sense that we might take for granted critical elements that the reader needs to know. This is why it's so important for us to continue to check that every line functions as intended.

Here's a simple revision of the previous line that captures the missing information:

```
        KARA scans the crowd for JANELLE, spots her dancing, and can't
        take her eyes off her.
```

In this next example of underwriting, we've left clues to suggest a particular conclusion but it falls short of our intended meaning:

```
        Betty walks away from the building. Suddenly, she realizes
        something. She returns to the guard at the front entrance.
                            BETTY
                Can I get back inside real quick?
```

Try to forget everything you know about Betty's story and read what this text actually says: A character named Betty walks away from a building, realizes something, goes back, and asks permission to re-enter.

What has Betty realized that makes her want to go back inside? It's not clear. Dropping clues is great, but we need to be sure that the reader can discover the treasure at the end of the hunt. In this case, we need the reader to know that Betty left her purse. By adding a few details to clarify her actions, goal, and the setting, our new draft reads as follows:

```
Betty walks away from the club. She pats her shoulder searching
for something. No luck. She stops dead. Then sprints to the
bouncer at the front entrance.

                        BETTY
            I left my purse inside--can I go
            grab it?
```

It's clear now that we're at a club. Betty takes specific actions like patting her shoulder that offer direct clues to the reader that something is amiss. Lastly, she approaches the bouncer and names exactly what it is she's looking for.

EXERCISE: Did You Throw out the Baby with the Bathwater?

You know way more about your characters, scene, and story than your reader, and yet you must pretend you know nothing so that you can understand your scene from an uninformed reader's perspective.

The first part of this exercise is to identify and write down the key pieces of information that your reader *must* glean from your scene. As a starting place, let's look back to the elements that we deemed so important during Part I, namely:

Character(s)

Setting and Time

Motivation

Scene Goal

Obstacle(s)

Approach(es)

Resolution

Not all of this material comes up in every scene, of course, but some subset must be at play in the draft you're working with. Go through item by item and explicitly list the information that the scene is meant to convey.

In Betty's case, for example, our list might look something like:

Character(s): Betty and the bouncer.

Setting and Time: Miami dance club, night.

Motivation: Betty wants her money and ID back so she can get home.

Scene Goal: Get her purse from inside the club.

Obstacle(s): The bouncer.

Approach(es): Betty asks nicely but he says no. Then she tries charming him, but he doesn't bite.

Once you've made your list, look at the scene itself. Start with the raw materials: setting, time, and *dramatis personae*. Circle the actual line or lines in your script where each of these elements is presented to your reader. If you can't find the line, then it's underwritten. Add it. But even if the line's there, confirm that what you have written is clear enough for a reader to understand. Revise where necessary.

Next read through the rest of the list and circle the line(s) in your scene that deliver each of the relevant pieces of information. Where exactly does Kara ask Janelle to dance? Where does Detective Shovel actually search for clues? Where does Betty actually ask the bouncer if she can go back inside the club to find her purse? Where does he reject her? If you don't find the precise line, add it. And if you do find the line, make sure that it's clear and appropriately informative.

If you're using the treasure hunt strategy from Chapter 6, make sure that the hints you've left add up to the conclusion you intend. Isolate the specific clues and read them sequentially. Is it clear? If not, revise accordingly.

And remember: your reader has never read your scene before and might never read it again. So use this opportunity to make sure they know everything you need them to know.

10 Managing Scene Information in Dialogue

In most films and shows, characters go about their business with no idea they're being watched by an audience through what's often referred to as an invisible *fourth wall*. For this dynamic to function, the characters must say and do things that make sense in the absence of the audience. If they don't, it breaks the illusion of the fourth wall and sounds unnatural, as in the following exchange:

```
                    MRS. BARRETT
          Hurry, Rose, we have to prepare
          the house for our distinguished,
          handsome, and influential guest.

                    ROSE
          Yes, Mother, I know our guest is
          coming and I'm excited to meet
          him.

                    MRS. BARRETT
          He is the last suitor. As you
          know, if he doesn't propose, our
          fortunes are ruined. We will be
          destitute.

                    ROSE
          Oh, Mother, he's our one remaining
          chance. I am so worried he won't
          propose!
```

Yikes. Clearly, Mrs. Barrett and her daughter already know the suitor is coming, that their fortunes are in peril, and that the suitor is their last, best chance. There's no reason for them to repeat this information to each other, except as a way for the writer to convey it to the reader. When story information is forced out like this in a blatant fourth wall-breaking way, it's called *obvious exposition*.

But the exposition is not just obvious in the above example, it's also repetitive. Rose and Mrs. Barrett are listening attentively to each other, so there's no reason for them to re-state facts that have just been delineated. It's another violation of the authenticity of their conversation to do so, and it's mind-numbing for the reader. This unnecessarily echoed information is *redundant exposition*.

When exposition is obvious or redundant, the expository tail is wagging the dialogue dog. It should be the other way around. To honor the fourth wall, characters must have convincing conversations in and of themselves. Any exposition that emerges must do so naturally and realistically.

This is not to say that that dialogue itself must be "realistic" or "naturalistic," it need only follow the rules of naturalism. The dialogue in a film like THE PRINCESS BRIDE is deliberately stylized like a YA fantasy novel, the dialogue in SCOTT PILGRIM VS. THE WORLD is infused with inflections of gaming and pop culture, and the dialogue in MOONRISE KINGDOM is decidedly earnest and adult even when the characters aren't. But the writers of these films still found ways to have their stylized dialogue offer up believable exposition instead of forcing it onto their readers.

When dialogue is labored and is used as a blunt instrument to unload story information, it can alienate readers from experiencing the story. So how do you respect the fourth wall and still inform your reader? That's what this short but important chapter is all about.

As You Know, I'm Your Son

To write dialogue without obvious exposition, you must create a compelling reason for your characters to discuss the information you need your reader to learn. Below we describe three common ways to create this credible pretext: by creating conflict around the subject, by establishing a disparity of knowledge between the characters, or by having characters acknowledge that they are stating the obvious.

I'm So Conflicted

In case you've missed it, conflict is all over this book. As we introduced in Part I, stories are driven by characters trying to get what they want and being thwarted by obstacles. What does that create? Conflict.

The good news is that conflict between two characters creates a wonderful opportunity for exposition to emerge. Suppose we have a sister and brother, and it's an important story point for the reader to know their mother's name. This information would be so basic to the two of them that they would never come right out and say it:

```
                    SISTER
          Our mother, Ellen, called last
          night.

                    BROTHER
          What did she want?
```

The "Ellen" is inserted only for the reader's benefit. It sounds false because it is. If the siblings are going to speak her name, the writer needs a pretext to make it sound natural. One great way to do this is to create conflict around the name itself:

```
                    SISTER
          You said Ellen had stopped
          drinking.

                    BROTHER
          Don't call her Ellen.

                    SISTER
          That's her name, isn't it?

                    BROTHER
          She's our mother, call her mom—

                    SISTER
          You can call her whatever you
          want. To me she's Ellen.
```

In this case, we've given the siblings a mutually exclusive desire revolving around this piece of expository information. Brother wants Sister to use the term "mom," Sister wants to refer to her as "Ellen." As a result, it's perfectly natural for her name to come up. Their particular goals about their mother's name may not be their scene goals, but they work in these few lines of dialogue to deliver the necessary exposition.

In LITTLE MISS SUNSHINE (page 13), writer Michael Arndt needs to deliver an important piece of exposition to the reader that the characters already know, namely, that Grandpa was kicked out of his previous retirement home. To deliver this information to the reader, Arndt slips it into a conflict over that night's dinner:

                    GRANDPA
          [...] Is it possible, just one
          time, we could have something for
          dinner except the goddamn fucking
          chicken?!

Sheryl ignores him. Richard tries to cut him off.

                    RICHARD
          Dad... Dad... Dad... Dad!!!

                    GRANDPA
          I'm just saying...!

                    RICHARD
          If you want to cook or buy your
          own food, you're more than
          welcome...

                    GRANDPA
          Christ. Y'know, at Sunset
          Village...

                    RICHARD
          If you liked Sunset Village so
          much maybe you shouldn't have
          gotten yourself kicked out of
          there...!

On page 27 of THE WAY WAY BACK, Trent and Kip disagree about whether Duncan should wear a life vest. The important story information emerging from their conflict is that Trent doesn't actually care if Duncan can swim or not; he just doesn't want to have to worry about him. Co-writers Nat Faxon and Jim Rash use a super uncool, horribly embarrassing life vest as a contested object to make Trent's lack of concern for Duncan's feelings evident:

```
                    TRENT
          You need to wear that.

                    KIP
          Oh, I think he's cool without it.

                    TRENT
          No, Duncan can't swim.

                    PAM
                (trying to make it better,
                 clarifying)
          Trent, he's just not a comfortable
          swimmer.

                    KIP
          I really think he'll be fine.

                    TRENT
          No, let's wear it, buddy. So,
          people don't have to worry about
          you, right?
```

In this situation, not everyone knows about Duncan's swimming ability. But the conflict over the life vest gives it a logical reason to become a part of the conversation.

In BOOKSMART, Molly confronts Jared about his over-the-top graduation party, which becomes a pretext to reveal information about their relationship (page 38):

```
     Molly gestures around the room--

                    MOLLY
          Dude, this doesn't work. You
          can't...buy people's affection.

                    JARED
          I'm pretty sure you can. I've seen
          it a lot. My parents did. Their
          parents did.

                    MOLLY
          Just-- stop trying so hard. It's
          embarrassing. People can sense it,
          and it turns them off.

                    JARED
          But you try hard. You try hard at
          everything. That's what I like
          about you.
```

Their disagreement about money's influence provides an opportunity for Jared to finally tell Molly that he likes her.

Do You Know Why I Pulled You Over?

Another powerful way to deliver exposition without breaking the scenic integrity of a conversation is to create a situation where one character knows more than the other. Creating a *disparity of knowledge* between two characters provides a perfectly realistic opportunity for one to teach the other, and for the readers to learn along with them.

Let's imagine we need to communicate to the reader that two siblings have recently attended a funeral. The siblings already know they were there, of course, which means that they're not likely to discuss that fact with each other. But if we create a disparity in their knowledge of the event, it opens up a great opportunity to deliver needed exposition:

```
                    SISTER
          Did you check out what he was
          wearing?

                    BROTHER
          Uncle Bob?

                    SISTER
          Who chose an open casket?

                    BROTHER
          At least we'll never have to see
          that tie again.
```

This exchange informs the reader about Uncle Bob's funeral without ever mentioning it directly. It works on the idea that even though they were both in the same space at the same time, the sister doesn't know if her brother saw Bob's mortal remains. She wants to find out, so she asks, and voilà, it's a perfectly natural thing to discuss.

Exploiting a disparity of knowledge is a very common tool for conveying exposition. Here's an example from THE INCREDIBLES (page 18).

```
                    PRINCIPAL
          I appreciate you coming down here
          so quickly, Mrs. Parr.

Helen enters and takes a seat. Dash stares at the floor.

                    HELEN
          What's this all about? Has Dash
          done something wrong?

                    KROPP
          He's a disruptive influence. And
          he openly mocks me in front of the
          class.

                    DASH
          He says.

                    KROPP
          I know it's you!!
              (to Helen)
          He puts thumbtacks on my stool!
```

In this scene, the Principal, Dash, and Dash's teacher Kropp all know why Dash is in trouble. But Helen (Dash's mom) doesn't. And since we get to hear the same explanation that Helen asks for, it doesn't feel like the characters are only speaking for our benefit.

Helen is a new arrival in the above scene. Her role as outsider creates a perfect pretext for the writer to provide information to her and the reader. Characters like the rookie cop, the private, the new kid in school, or the recent arrival will find themselves in situations where they have to rely on someone with more information (like the captain, the teacher, the doctor, the news anchor, the chief, the senior, the old salt, etc.) to get them up to speed.

Here's an apt example of a new arrival needing further explanation from MANCHESTER BY THE SEA by Kenneth Lonergan. Lee finds out his brother has fallen ill. He races to the hospital, only to learn that it's too late. His brother is dead. On page 11 Lee, along with the reader, finds out why:

```
                    LEE
          Where's my brother?

                    DR MULLER
          He's downstairs. You can see him
          if you want.

                    LEE
          What happened?

                    DR MULLER
          Well, you know his heart was very
          weak at this point, and it just
          gave out. If it's any comfort, I
          don't think he suffered very much.
```

In a scene from QUEEN & SLIM (page 27), a sheriff happens to be the one who is less informed, so he asks a dispatcher for details about the recent cop killing:

```
                    SHERIFF
          What kind of car were they in?

                    VOICE
          A white Honda.

                    SHERIFF
          Any other info?

                    VOICE
          We're still waiting for the dash
          cam footage to come in.
```

The new expository information that emerges for the reader is that the dash camera footage is not yet in. Which is good news for Queen and Slim, at least for now.

In Eric Heisserer's script for ARRIVAL, linguist Louise is up for an important government job. Even though she is highly qualified, Colonel Weber won't hire her because she's making too many demands. To demonstrate that a different candidate (Danvers) is less qualified, Louise suggests that Weber ask Danvers about the Sanskrit word for "war" and its definition. In the next scene (page 15), Weber returns:

```
            COLONEL WEBER
Good morning.

            LOUISE
Colonel?

            COLONEL WEBER
Gavisti.

            LOUISE
That's the word. But what did
Danvers say it means in Sanskrit?

            COLONEL WEBER
He said it means an argument.
What does it really mean?

            LOUISE
"A desire for more cows."

            COLONEL WEBER
Pack your bags.
```

The exchange demonstrates in no uncertain terms that Louise is the better linguist. This is the exposition the reader (and Colonel Weber) needs to know. As a result, she lands the job.

Thank You, Captain Obvious

If a character discloses obvious exposition, but in doing so demonstrates brazen self-awareness of the fact, it can provide a credible pretext for the information. In other words, if you make it clear to your readers that the character is acting knowingly, readers will accept the new information as consistent with the idea of the fourth wall. Consider the following example:

```
            MRS. BARRETT
Are you at all aware who is about
to arrive?

            ROSE
Is he a distinguished, handsome,
and influential guest?

            MRS. BARRETT
This is important. Please, try to
be serious.
```

Mrs. Barrett's response to Rose signals to the reader that Rose's line was spoken sarcastically. Because Rose is self-aware of her own obvious exposition, she can get away with a line that in other, more sincere circumstances, would ring false. Note that a wrylie could also be used in this case to indicate Rose's sarcasm.

Here is another example in which one character calls out another's self-awareness for the benefit of the reader:

```
                    SISTER
          Remember how I said I was worried
          that mom would embarrass us at the
          wake?

                    BROTHER
          Like, this morning?

                    SISTER
          Yeah?

                    BROTHER
          Are you seriously asking me if I
          remember what you said this
          morning?
```

Sister's first line comes dangerously close to being obvious exposition, but Brother's response makes it clear that her line was actually about him paying (or not paying) attention to her.

Below is a great illustration of this approach from BOOKSMART (page 21). The writers want to emphasize that Molly has spent her high school years methodically pursuing a career path instead of enjoying herself. Amy would already know this, of course, so how can Molly still say it in a way that sounds authentic? Consider: The fact that Molly's dialogue devolves into awkward self-awareness makes it fit the situation. She realizes she's oversold her point, and says so.

```
                    MOLLY
          I'm serious, Amy. Everyone thinks
          we're these robots. They think all
          we care about is taking a million
          APs and getting into Yale and
          editing Law Review at Georgetown
          and clerking for a Federal Judge
          between Junior and Senior Year
          before eventually being the
          youngest justice ever nominated to
          the Supreme Court of the United
          States!
                    (then, awkwardly)
          In my case. You get my point. No
          one knows we can be fun too.
```

EXERCISE: Un-obviousing Your Exposition

Go over your scene and highlight every bit of exposition that comes through dialogue. You're looking for all the pieces of story information that are critical for your readers to understand what happens in your scene.

For each highlighted line, ask yourself: is this information that the conversational partner already knows? If so, reframe the conversation using a conflict, disparity of knowledge, or self-awareness to convey the information with greater authenticity. The conversation must sound plausible in the absence of a reader.

Yeah, You Already Said That

Another form of exposition to remove from your dialogue is *redundant exposition*. In other words, don't have your characters tell your readers things they already know. Show your readers that you value their time and attention by making a point clearly and then moving on.

This is more than just an information issue, it's a trust issue. If you treat your readers like the clever, thoughtful, aware people that they are, then they'll reward that trust with their attention.

Here We Are in Prison

One common form of redundant exposition is when visual information is unnecessarily repeated in dialogue. Take, for example, the location of your scene. It appears in the slugline and will be seen by your reader so it need not be re-articulated by your character, as in the following example:

```
INT. APARTMENT HALLWAY - CRIME SCENE

Shovel stands with his partner facing an apartment door blocked
off with caution tape.

                    SHOVEL
          So, this is where it happened.
```

To avoid redundant exposition like this, if a character references the setting, their comment should add new information that pushes the story forward. For example:

```
INT. APARTMENT HALLWAY - CRIME SCENE

Shovel stands with his partner facing an apartment door blocked
off with caution tape.

                    SHOVEL
          Forensics dusted for prints, so
          it's all ours.
```

Keep your eye out for expressions that start with, "Oh look.." and "Here we are…." and "Isn't that …?" because they're prone to repeating information from the slugline: "Oh look, the Eiffel Tower!" and "Here's the beach!" and "Isn't that the club we're going to?"

In addition to not repeating obvious information from the slugline, you also want to look out for information from scene description that's plainly repeated in dialogue, such as:

```
    Detective Shovel scours every corner of the crime scene. He
    comes up empty-handed. The Chief enters.

                        CHIEF
              Whaddya got?

                        DETECTIVE SHOVEL
              I couldn't find anything.
```

Readers know that he didn't find anything, so Shovel might as well skip past the obvious and jump to the next step in the investigation:

```
    Detective Shovel scours every corner of the crime scene. He
    comes up empty-handed. The Chief enters.

                        CHIEF
              Whaddya got?

                        DETECTIVE SHOVEL
              Please, tell me you have other
              leads.
```

Conversely, if there is important information that you'd like to communicate through dialogue, make sure you cull any redundancies from your scene description. Here's an example from EIGHTH GRADE in which a key piece of story information emerges in dialogue instead of scene description (page 70):

```
    Aniyah is staring off at something in the distance, looking
    weirded out.

                        ANIYAH
              Okay, like, don't all look at the
              same time but like some creepy ass
              dude has been staring at us for
              five minutes acting like he's not.
              [...]
```

The line of scene description preceding Aniyah's dialogue doesn't say anything about what she's staring at. Instead, it's up to her dialogue to provide the new (and therefore not redundant) exposition. In this particular case, the creepy dude turns out to be Kayla's dad trying to surreptitiously check in on his daughter. To have identified him explicitly in scene description would have spoiled the reveal. Instead, Burnham maintains the mystery for the reader (as he does for Aniyah) until Kayla figures out who she sees.

That's My Name, Don't Wear It Out

Another all-too-common form of redundant information is *name-calling*. As it turns out, people (and therefore characters) rarely do this. It may happen at the beginning of a phone conversation as a means of identification, or as a point of emphasis, as in:

```
                      DAD
           Arjun, get back here this minute!
```

But in most circumstances we all simply speak to one another without using names. In fact, there are entire scripts in which characters' names are never spoken in dialogue (THE ROAD by Joe Penhall and THE DRIVER by Walter Hill, for example).

New scenewriters may wonder how their readers will know who everyone is if other characters don't keep saying their names out loud, but they don't have to. And indeed, it can get a little weird when they do.

Here's a short sample from MOONRISE KINGDOM (page 21) the way it was written:

```
Sam and Suzy face each other in the wide meadow. Sam says
carefully:

                        SAM
                Were you followed?

                        SUZY
                    (looking around)
                I doubt it.

                        SAM
                Good.
```

Now notice how awkward (and weirdly intense) the same dialogue becomes if names are added:

```
Sam and Suzy face each other in the wide meadow. Sam says
carefully:

                        SAM
                Were you followed, Suzy?

                        SUZY
                    (looking around)
                I doubt it, Sam.

                        SAM
                Good, Suzy.
```

Your reader will know the name of whoever is talking because it'll be printed right there above every block of their dialogue. There's no need to repeat it in dialogue without good reason.

EXERCISE: Removing Redundant Exposition

Reread the sluglines for your scene and all relevant scene descriptions referring to the location. Now check your dialogue for lines that also refer to the location. Cut any redundant observations, or revise them to add new information. Conversely, if you want the observation to emerge in dialogue only, be sure to cut any preceding reference from your scene description so that the dialogue is not redundant.

Cut all name-calling from your dialogue unless there's a specific narrative reason to include it, like one character trying to get another's attention, or as a point of emphasis or sarcasm. Or just try pulling the name-calling entirely and see how it reads.

Cut any lines of dialogue that repeat facts or circumstances that have already been mentioned. If you are adding new information, that's one thing, but if your dialogue only serves to remind the reader of something they know, then you don't need it.

11 Bringing Authenticity into Your Dialogue

Have you ever played chess? Fun game, you should check it out. The idea, of course, is that every turn you get the chance to move one piece to improve your position, with the aim of capturing the opposing king.

Now imagine playing chess against yourself.

If you want it to be a good game, one that is balanced and fair, every time you move a white piece you have to fully engage as that player. When you're pushing white pieces you want white to win. When you turn the board around and move a black piece, you have to change your mindset and do your absolute best to win as black. Whatever color you represent in the moment, that's your team, and you must play that truth.

Dialogue is exactly the same. To write believable dialogue you have to be true and faithful to your character no matter who they are: benevolent, evil, misguided, villain, obstacle, heroine, antagonist. Whether they are distracted, angry, bored, anxious, grumpy, hungry, or elated, you must understand what they want and embody those desires in writing whatever it is that they're feeling and doing in the moment. And then you have to do the exact same thing for the other character(s). When you're playing black, play black. When you're playing white, play white.

The whole weird, oxymoronic task of dialogue is that you're trying to construct "real" dialogue. But of course, it's not real, it's crafted, and you have to play both sides without bias or your reader will sense the artifice. All the ideas covered in this chapter will help you write every participant in your scene's conversation with the full complexity that a real character deserves. Follow these leads, and your dialogue will naturally grow more compelling, engaging, and believable.

Keepin' It Real

Try to imagine the following: two people come together in conversation. They take turns speaking. They talk in clear statements and full sentences. They say exactly what they feel and exactly what they mean. They listen to each other carefully, and value what the other is saying. Any conflict they might have would get worked out in seconds:

```
                    BROTHER
          I'm unhappy that you ate my ice
          cream bar.

                    SISTER
          I'm sorry.

                    BROTHER
          I wish that you would respect my
          things.

                    SISTER
          I'll buy you a new ice cream and
          be more attentive in the future.
```

Maybe this kind of exchange could happen in a therapist's office. But out in the world? No way.

The difference is that real people, and three-dimensional characters, don't wait around just hoping someone will talk to them. They pursue their own thoughts, interests, and agendas. Characters will act and speak from their desires even when they are sympathetic to their conversational partner. To write realistic dialogue, therefore, you need to mimic that self-interest by understanding and expressing what each character wants.

The way these different desires manifest in fully rounded conversations is that characters speak in fragments, ask questions, interrupt and ignore each other, and do all the other things you'd expect from people who bring their own agendas to the table. Because of this, good dialogue is often a battle for air time.

Consider the following exchange from page 37 of THE INCREDIBLES between Bob Parr (Mr. Incredible) and his boss, Gilbert Huph:

```
            HUPH
    Look at me when I'm talking to
    you, Parr!

            BOB
        (pointing)
    That man out there-- he needs
    help!

            HUPH
    Do NOT change the subject, Bob!
    We're discussing your attitude!

            BOB
    But he's getting mugged!
```

Each character in this exchange has their own topic that presents an obstacle for the other. Huph is there to chastise Bob for undermining the company's bottom line. Bob wants to save the poor guy who is getting mugged outside. Their mutually exclusive desires put them into conflict. That conflict persists because they can't both get what they want.

If the main topic of your scene (the one pursued by your main character) is disrupted by another, that *off-topic* dialogue creates conflict. It serves as an obstacle. Consider the following:

```
            BETTY
    Hi, I was wondering if I could go
    inside real quick--

            BOUNCER
        (sipping a coffee)
    Yo, Derrick, you forgot the sugar.

            BETTY
    Sorry to interrupt, I left my
    purse--

            BOUNCER
    Two creamers and a sugar, how hard
    is that?
```

The bouncer's off-topic preoccupation with his coffee impedes Betty in the pursuit of her goal. From a conflict perspective, the more obstacles you have in a scene, the better. Furthermore, a good preoccupation like this one renders both the bouncer and his location with greater authenticity. The reader will intuit that the bouncer was just handed the wrong coffee. We don't see this happen, but it gestures towards a fully lived reality that the bouncer must have: he's busy doing his own thing, in his own space, instead of just waiting around to serve Betty's story needs.

When a character steers a conversation off-topic it creates the sense of an interior life for them, real and distinct from any other characters. In MOONRISE KINGDOM, Sam Shakusky, a twelve-year-old khaki scout, runs away from camp and is missing. In a subsequent scene (page 12), Scout Master Ward has assembled the other scouts to search for him:

```
                    SCOUT MASTER WARD
               You have your orders. Use the
               orienteering and path-finding
               skills you've been practicing all
               summer. Let's find our man and
               bring him safely back to camp.
               Remember: this isn't just a search
               party, it's a chance to do some
               first-class scouting. Any
               questions?

     Lazy-Eye raises his hand. Scout Master Ward points to him.

                    SCOUT MASTER WARD
               Lazy-Eye.

                    LAZY-EYE
               What's your real job, sir?

                    SCOUT MASTER WARD
                 (caught off-guard)
               I'm a math teacher.

                    LAZY-EYE
               What grade?

                    SCOUT MASTER WARD
                 (stiffening)
               Eighth. Why?

     Lazy-Eye shrugs. Scout Master Ward frowns.
```

Scout Master Ward has a kid missing. You don't have to be an expert on khaki scouting to imagine that's a pretty serious breach of responsibility. Ward urgently wants to find Sam. That is the reason they are assembled and it is the main topic of the scene. But like a typical kid, Lazy-Eye's got other things on his mind. His preoccupation with Ward's real job acts as an obstacle.

Lazy-Eye's off-topic goofiness stands in stark contrast to the dark, calculating mind of Rose in GET OUT. On page 66, Chris suspects the worst and wants Rose to leave with him. But knowing that Chris is beginning to see through her family's deception, Rose deliberately changes the topic to stall for time:

                              CHRIS
                    Let's go back home tonight.

                              ROSE
                    What? Wait, no.

                              CHRIS
                    I'm just... Something doesn't feel
                    right.

                              ROSE
                    You mean with us?

                              CHRIS
                    No. With this whole situation! I
                    just... I can't explain but I need
                    you to trust me. Let's just go. It
                    doesn't even have to be a big
                    deal.

                              ROSE
                    It is a big deal. It's my family.
                    I wouldn't even know what to tell
                    them.

And moments later:

```
                    ROSE
          Yes, it's weird. There are a lot
          of ways I wish this was going
          different. I wish my brother
          wasn't a cock. I wish my parents'
          friends were chill; but just
          because it's tough, it doesn't
          mean you run away...

     Rose cries.

                    CHRIS
          Baby, I--

                    ROSE
          ...I'm late.

                    CHRIS
          Late?

                    ROSE
          I should've got my period like
          last week.

                    CHRIS
          Oh.
```

Rose may be deceitful and horrible, but she's written with authenticity. Her masterful steering of the conversation towards a fake pregnancy is perfectly aligned with her desire to keep Chris in the dark.

In the above example, Chris tells Rose exactly what he wants. In dialogue, sometimes it's safer, or more strategic, or convenient to talk around a subject instead. Let's assume that we've set up that Kara is about to ask Janelle to dance. One way to present this moment is to show her simply walking up to Janelle and asking:

```
                    KARA
          Hi. Umm, would you like to dance?
```

But anyone who's lived through middle school knows that this is a lot harder to do than it is to write. If Kara's nervous, worried about rejection, not sure what to say, or feeling hesitant for any other reason, then she might begin with an off-topic question to lead up to it:

```
                         KARA
              Don't you love this song?
```

Maybe not the most original line in the world, but it opens the conversation with her crush on safer terrain and could easily become a bridge to the primary topic later on. In other words, her off-topic question is still a step towards her goal of asking Janelle to dance. It's not random. It forwards the story and comes from a place that's true to her character.

I'm Listening

In addition to whatever topics come up in conversation, you also need to be mindful of how carefully each character listens to what others are saying. You have the freedom to have a character hang on every word, cherry-pick only what they want to hear, or completely ignore the speaker (in which case the two characters *talk in parallel*). In keeping with the theme of this section, the choice of how much someone is listening must be authentic to their character and reflective of their current internal state.

Here's an example from SCOTT PILGRIM VS. THE WORLD (page 12) of a character not listening at all. Scott and his girlfriend Knives are in a record store. Knives is fan-girling so hard over a CD that she's oblivious to what Scott is saying:

```
                    KNIVES CHAU
            Oh, I heart them so much.

                    SCOTT
            I hearted them too until they
            signed to a major label and the
            singer turned into a total bitch
            and ruined my life. But that's
            just me.

                    KNIVES CHAU
                (oblivious)
            Envy Adams is sooo cool. Do you
            read her blog?
```

Throughout the same film, Scott doesn't pick up on the many times Ramona corrects his use of the term "ex-boyfriends," as on page 77. Preoccupied with keeping them together, Scott cherry-picks from what Ramona is saying to him:

```
                    RAMONA
            Yeah, I do that. Listen, I know
            it's hard to be around me
            sometimes. I'll understand if you
            don't want to hang anymore.

                    SCOTT
            No. No, I want to hang. The whole
            evil ex-boyfriend thing. No
            biggie.

                    RAMONA
            Exes.

                    SCOTT
            I mean, I know it's early days,
            but I don't think anything can
            really get in the way of how I...
```

Even if every character is listening to each other perfectly, their individual interests must remain clear in the writer's mind. If not, the danger is that one character will serve only as a foil for the other's concerns.

SceneWriting

The following scene from THE INCREDIBLES (page 106) features a single topic and attentive listening by both parties. The dialogue works, however, because they have clear, mutually exclusive goals: Frozone wants to hop into battle and save the city. But his wife, Honey, is prepping for their upcoming dinner party:

<pre>
                        FROZONE
          Honey?

                        HONEY'S VOICE
          What?

                        FROZONE
          Where's my supersuit?

                        HONEY'S VOICE
          What?

                        FROZONE
          WHERE. IS. MY. SUPER. SUIT?!

                        HONEY'S VOICE
          I put it away.

                        FROZONE
          WHERE?!

                        HONEY'S VOICE
          Why do you need to know?

                        FROZONE
          I NEED it!
</pre>

Honey hears and understands Frozone perfectly. She knows before he says it that if he's asking for his supersuit it means her dinner party is imperiled. Her separate interest—preserving her evening—comes across loud and clear in the way she avoids answering his questions.

Speaking of Questions . . .

You may notice in the exchange above that there are seven questions asked in nine lines. The effect of asking literal questions in dialogue is that they can help make characters appear distinct and dimensional. When Frozone asks for his supersuit and Honey replies, "Why do you need to know?" it's clear she's skeptical about his intentions. Her reply indicates that she's not only heard his question, but understands its implications vis-à-vis her own goals. This skepticism renders Honey as a fully rounded character rather than an arbitrary obstacle that only exists to impede Frozone. Not bad for one line of dialogue.

EXERCISE: Going Off-Topic and Ignoring

Read through your scene's dialogue as it is currently written, and for each line of dialogue do the following:

1   Circle the line if it's about the main character's primary topic of conversation, and

2   Draw a star next to the line if it shows that the speaker was listening to everything the last speaker just said.

Before you get into making any changes, you may spot some interesting patterns in your dialogue simply by measuring these qualities. If everything is circled, then everyone is talking about the same thing. If there are a lot of stars, then everyone is listening perfectly to everyone else. If you didn't intend either of those effects, then mix it up to create contrast and keep things fresh.

If you see lots of circles, brainstorm ways to get the conversation off-topic. What actions might your characters be involved in when the scene begins? What preoccupations might they have? These could be setting-specific, like clearing a table at a restaurant or helping a customer at a retail store. Or a character might simply have another topic on their mind. Maybe they're distracted by the big game, their pending divorce, or the rock stuck in their shoe.

Come up with three to five things that each character would have on their mind besides the topic that the main character wants to discuss. Consider ideas that are revealing of character, connect to the larger story, and can act as conversational obstacles for the main character to overcome.

Choosing the best of your brainstormed topics, insert responses from your secondary characters that bring to life these off-topic subjects.

Now consider how a competing topic impacts everyone's tendency to listen. With multiple topics at play, are your characters ignoring, cherry-picking, or paying very close attention to what's being said? Breaking out of the pattern of perfect listening will ensure that each character has a real agenda. It will create conflict, and develop secondary characters who don't exist simply so the main character has someone to talk to.

Read Between the Lines

People want what they want, but they also want to keep the peace, their friends, their jobs, and their health. So instead of saying exactly what they mean, they hedge, deflect, talk around things, and in general rely on *subtext* so as not to disrupt their lives and reputations.

At the end of WHEN HARRY MET SALLY (page 120), writer Nora Ephron has Harry finally declare his love for Sally. The reader has been rooting for those two crazy kids to get together the entire script, and here is the moment when it should finally happen. Harry spots Sally across a crowded room, rushes up to her, and delivers an impassioned speech about all many the reasons he wants to be with her, ending with:

```
                HARRY
      [...] I came here tonight because
      when you realize that you want to
      spend the rest of your life with
      somebody, you want the rest of
      your life to start as soon as
      possible.
```

She clearly loves him, too, so it's a done deal, right? She'll tell him and they'll ride off into the sunset. Not so fast:

```
                SALLY
      See, that's just like you, Harry.
      You say things like that, and you
      make it impossible for me to hate
      you --
           (almost in tears)
      And I hate you. I hate you, Harry,
      I hate you.
```

Wait … What? How can she hate him? Oh, hold on, the scene isn't over yet …

```
She starts to cry.

Harry puts his arms around her.

They kiss.

A long kiss.

The twinkle ball goes around, twinkling.

They go on kissing.
```

The literal *text* of Sally's dialogue delivers one message: "I hate you, Harry."

But the implied subtext of what she really means—the message that comes through loud and clear thanks to Sally's tears and their extended kiss—is the opposite: "I love you, Harry."

Subtext is the implied message that differs from the literal meaning of the words a character actually says.

There's no subtext if a character says, "You make great cupcakes," and munches down another. If they say, "You make great cupcakes," while surreptitiously tossing one out the window, there's subtext. "Can I call you sometime?" followed by "Sure, here's my number" has no subtext. "Can I call you sometime?" followed by "I'm in the phone book" adds subtext.

People use subtext all the time, consciously and unconsciously, so adding subtext to your dialogue will lend your characters more authenticity. Furthermore, subtext is a powerful tool for reader engagement because it immediately puts readers onto a treasure hunt (see Chapter 6). When there's a discrepancy between what is said and what is meant, it's a clue to readers that things are not what they seem. Such dialogue invites interrogation and demands attention. It's the opposite of "on the nose" writing that says exactly what it means and therefore needs no interpretation by the reader.

Using Subtext to Avoid Hurt Feelings

Sometimes the truth hurts. Picture a dad driving his daughter to soccer practice:

> DAUGHTER
> Let me out here.
>
> DAD
> The field is three blocks away.
>
> DAUGHTER
> It's just that I don't want to be
> seen with you.

Harsh. If the daughter doesn't want to hurt her dad's feelings, but still wants to get dropped off early, she might deliver the same message through subtext:

> DAUGHTER
> I can get out here.
>
> DAD
> The field is three blocks away.
>
> DAUGHTER
> I like the walk.
>
> DAD
> Don't want to be seen with your
> dad?
>
> DAUGHTER
> It'll give me a chance to warm up.

Subtext inserts a nice layer of conflict to the scene: Will Dad accept her softer "warm up" excuse or will he force the issue even though she doesn't want to talk about it?

On page 6 of SELMA, written by Paul Webb and Ava DuVernay, Annie Lee Cooper tries to register to vote, but she faces a racist registrar:

```
                    REGISTRAR
            You work for Mr. Dunn at the rest
            home, ain't that right?

                    ANNIE LEE COOPER
                 (hesitantly)
            Yessir.

                    REGISTRAR
            Wonder what ol' Dunn'll say when I
            tell him one of his gals over here
            stirrin' trouble.

                    ANNIE LEE COOPER
            Ain't stirrin' trouble. I'm here
            to vote.
```

The registrar doesn't want Ms. Cooper to vote, but he can't legally stop her either. He threatens her job instead, in subtext. To do so explicitly would be illegal, and he knows it. Officially he's just "wondering" out loud what her boss might say, but it's very clear that he knows Ms. Cooper, where she works, who she works for, and he believes that her boss will punish her if he gets word.

In contrast, Ms. Cooper's dialogue is entirely without subtext. This is not an accident. Knowing the danger of the situation, clarity is essential to her character and must be a part of her approach to getting what she wants. The parenthetical comment "hesitantly" signals the reader that Ms. Cooper is aware of the registrar's threat. She's onto his subtextual meaning, which is why she takes extra pains to clarify that she's not causing any trouble at all, only exercising her rights.

Off-Topic Subtext

When something can't be spoken about directly, people will often substitute a safer off-topic subject instead. It might be that the real topic is inappropriate or taboo, it could be too emotionally loaded, or perhaps it's triggering or unsafe. Whatever the case, the idea is to find something less fraught, less difficult, or less dangerous that can be spoken about freely, even though those involved know what's *really* being discussed.

Imagine heading to another soccer practice with our dad and his embarrassed daughter:

```
                    DAD
          Want to hop out here?

                    DAUGHTER
          Thanks, Dad.

                    DAD
          I used to warm up before practice,
          too.

                    DAUGHTER
               (surprised)
          Really?

                    DAD
          Can you imagine being dropped off
          by your grandmother?
```

In this case, dad uses the off-topic of "warming up" to discuss the real topic of "not being embarrassed by one's parents." He can thank his daughter for offering him this gentle code in their previous scene.

If you have a scene where two people must talk about something that they can't (or don't want to) openly discuss, where should you look to find suitable off-topics?

One idea is to substitute the loaded topic with an analogous, easier-to-discuss subject. Let's say there are two characters who are having trouble discussing a gravely ill friend. Instead of talking about her head-on, they might instead discuss a dying houseplant, or a broken dish, or a day coming to an end. The trick is to find an analogous relationship between subjects. A messy room could stand for bad performance in school. Burnt toast could stand for a couple's failing relationship. And warming up for practice could stand in for not wanting to be seen with your embarrassing dad.

A wonderful example of a subtextual subject comes in a scene from KIDDING (Season 1, Episode 7) written by Dave Holstein. Earlier in the series, Deirdre learned that her husband Scott had an affair with their daughter Maddy's piano teacher. They cancelled Maddy's piano lessons because of it. In this scene, Deirdre and Scott have a conversation about Maddy resuming piano lessons while Maddy is in the room.

```
                    DEIRDRE
          I've been thinking about this a
          lot, and I feel that... if it
          would make you happier for... M--
          Maddy to take piano again, then
          she should take piano, and I'll
          just deal with it.

                    SCOTT
          Oh.

                    DEIRDRE
          She seemed happier.

                    SCOTT
          I don't think that's true. Plus,
          she's getting so good at clarinet.

                    MADDY
          I am?

                    DEIRDRE
          Yes honey.
```

Obviously, the piano stands in for his affair and the clarinet for his marriage. The result allows them to safely discuss their complex relationship issues in front of Maddy.

Using Subtext to Communicate Emotions

Imagine a kid who's angry that it's the first day of school and taking it out on his mom as he makes lunch:

```
          KID
You bought chunky peanut butter?
Seriously?

          MOM
Are you mad at me?

          KID
What? No.

          MOM
Then why are you yelling at me
about your lunch?
```

The kid might figure it out in the moment, or he might storm off to school with an unsatisfying sandwich. Regardless, he's not upset with his mom, he's angry about school. And that anger comes out unconsciously through his preoccupation with making lunch. We (and Mom) infer the subtext from her son's incongruous words and actions.

When a character says things like "I'm angry," "I'm so happy," or "I'm really sad," it may very well be true, but it's telling the reader what to think instead of showing them. Instead, your characters should *live their emotions*. Their words and actions should be reflective of their emotional state rather than descriptive of it. This asks the reader and the other characters in the conversation to deduce the emotions for themselves.

On page 81 of THE INCREDIBLES, Violet and Dash are terrified in the wake of their plane getting shot down. They don't say so directly, but it still comes through loud and clear:

```
          VIOLET & DASH
Mom! What're we gonna do? What're
we gonna do?
```

On page 62 of EIGHTH GRADE, Kayla's new high school friend invites her to the mall. Kayla is so ecstatic she can't control herself:

```
Kayla stops, hangs up the phone, rips her earbuds out, and
FREAKS - doing little hops, exhaling, breathing heavy. So
excited.

                    KAYLA
          OhmygodohmygodohmygodOHMYGOD.
```

On page 84 of BOOKSMART, Amy is angry and hurt after a huge fight with Molly. She storms into a bathroom for some privacy but stumbles into Hope, who incisively reads into Amy's uncharacteristic rudeness:

```
Amy jumps -- Hope is sitting on the toilet, smoking a joint.
                    HOPE
          I locked that.

                    AMY
                  (sharply)
          I guess you didn't.

                    HOPE
          What's wrong with you? Fight with
          your wife?
```

In all these cases the characters are living their emotional states. How they are feeling emerges in the combination of their words and actions, rather than being spoken directly.

EXERCISE: What I Mean Is . . .

This exercise explores three different ways to add subtext to a conversation. They may not all be appropriate for what you're doing with your scene, but give them all a try and go with what works best.

First, look for places in your scene where characters say exactly what they mean and instead have them substitute a new line for the intention. Remember that people often elide their true desires in conversations because it's less risky:

```
                    KARA
          Don't you love this song?
```

Second, find places in your scene where characters state their feelings, and replace them with lines that evoke their emotions. Instead of:

```
                    DETECTIVE SHOVEL
          It's so frustrating I can't find
          my phone!
```

Try:

```
                    DETECTIVE SHOVEL
          They can put a computer into a
          little box, why can't they put a
          freaking leash on it for God's
          sake?
```

Finally, consider changing who is there and/or where they are so that your characters can no longer speak freely. In other words, force them into having a coded conversation. Instead of:

```
                    BOUNCER
          I'd be happy to let you in but I
          don't want to get fired.
```

Try:

```
                BOUNCER
     My man Derrick let someone skip
     the line last week. Hey, Reg,
     where's D workin' now?

                REG
     He ain't.

                BOUNCER
           (to Betty)
     Did I mention Reg is my boss?
```

You Sound Just Like My Mom

The words real people use in conversation emerge from a mixture of their past (background, training, education, upbringing) and their present (who are they talking to, and in what context). So why should your characters be any different?

If Betty is a Cuban immigrant with a PhD in Neuroscience, she will sound very different than if she is a white suburban high school teenager. Moreover, if she is talking to her baby brother over a family dinner about his driving test, she will sound very different than if she is participating in a job interview at a new lab.

To have a clear understanding of how your character's background affects their language, especially if that background is different from your own, you'll need to do your research. Listen to the appropriate regional dialects, take into account character age, education, and look for specialized language that is applicable to their occupation(s).

But also recognize that you shouldn't overdo it. Your objective is clarity. Dropping in a word or two of vernacular, using local slang, or spelling a word phonetically can be useful in moderation, but if you write every line to emphasize these distinctions it will get old and unreadable real fast.

One line like this is all you need to establish that someone is a doctor:

```
                    DOCTOR
          Looks like a subdural hematoma,
          but I don't see any complicating
          factors.
```

In truth, your character's background on a scene-to-scene basis is probably less important than the context of the conversation they're having. The same character may speak differently depending on their audience, the level of formality, the goal of the conversion, and any power dynamic that exists between them and their conversational partner.

A nice example of context changing a character's vocabulary appears in MOONRISE KINGDOM (page 22), when Sam realizes he's using Khaki Scout lingo with Suzy (who isn't a scout). He clarifies:

```
                    SAM
              (pointing on the map)
          Here's where we are right now. I'd
          like to pitch camp here by
          sixteen-hundred (which means four
          o'clock). How does that sound?
```

In SELMA, the character of Dr. King engages in dialogue with everyone from Presidents to advisors to congregations, family, and friends. His voice changes accordingly. First consider the following informal exchange with one of his advisors (page 8):

```
                    YOUNG
        [...] Also, I highly recommend you
        take this face-to-face opportunity
        to discuss Hoover. The
        surveillance...

                    KING
        Andy, I don't want to open that
        can, my friend.

                    YOUNG
        It's open, Marty. It's already
        open. Just a matter of when and
        how they want to spill it all out.
```

Notice how differently Dr. King spoke when accepting the Nobel Peace Prize a few pages earlier (page 5):

```
                    JAHN
        [...] To this undaunted champion
        of peace, the Nobel Committee of
        the Norwegian Parliament awards
        the Peace Prize for 1964. For you,
        sir.

    Visibly moved, King accepts and steps to the microphone.

                    KING
        Your Royal Highness, Mr.
        President, Excellencies. I refuse
        to accept that mankind is so bound
        to the starless midnight of racism
        that the bright daybreak of
        brotherhood can never be a
        reality. [...]
```

He's the same character, of course, but notice how the circumstances change not only what ideas are being expressed, but how. Dr. King's earlier informality comes out through the colloquial phrases "can of worms" and "my friend," while the grand audience and circumstances of the Nobel ceremony provide a forum for Dr. King's renowned lyrical and sublime language to shine.

EXERCISE: Finding Your Voice

Cover the names of the characters speaking in your scene, then read through everything they say. Are their voices distinct? Can you tell who is who based on their vocabulary choices, the urgency of their conversation, their formality, their dialect, or slang? Does one character have more power than the other? If you're finding it hard to tell your characters apart, then do what you can to infuse more of each character's voice into any ambiguous lines. Reveal your character not just through dialect but by how they'd choose to present themselves in the current conversational context.

The Rhythm Is Gonna Get You

There is music in great dialogue. Of course, the content of a given conversation serves critical expository and engagement goals in your scene, but without musicality you're going to have conversations that feel stiff, and unnatural. Consider a couple, Kiara and Li Wei, talking about dinner:

```
                    KIARA
          What do you think about pizza
          tonight?

                    LI WEI
          What tie do you like better?

                    KIARA
          I like the blue one better.

                    LI WEI
          I'm more in the mood for sushi.

                    KIARA
          Could you pick it up on your way
          home?
```

Based on what you've already read about dialogue in this chapter, this exchange has a lot going for it: each character has their own topic; the conversation starts with Kiara's subject then moves through a brief digression into Li Wei's before returning back to Kiara's; both characters use statements and questions; there isn't perfect listening.

Yet despite these positives, their exchange drags. They sound flat, monotonous, and straight-up boring. Where is that coming from?

A closer look reveals that each line of dialogue is about the same length (five to nine words). This alone has a huge impact on the atonality of their exchange. There are also a lot of repeated words that tend to blur rather than highlight the differences between the two characters.

To increase the musicality of an exchange, start by deleting repeated words (such as, in this case, "what," "better," "like," and even "I"). Mix up the line length by adding words to some lines and subtracting words from the others, and vary up the sentence length within individual lines. What those changes get you is something like this:

```
                        KIARA
            What do you think about pizza
            tonight?

                        LI WEI
            Which tie?

                        KIARA
            Blue.

                        LI WEI
            How about sushi? Osaka just
            reopened.

                        KIARA
            Think you could grab it on your
            way home?
```

Now we're getting somewhere. Musically, Kiara and Li Wei's voices play like two different instruments instead of one. There is rhythmic and verbal contrast. It sings.

Another way to bring rhythm in your dialogue is by inserting naturalistic tics. The next time you are in a public space like a café or restaurant take a moment to listen to someone else's conversation. Not the content so much, but how it is said. If you were to transcribe such an exchange (for purely academic purposes) what you'd find is that only rarely will one person speak a complete sentence without interruption. Moreover, speakers will pause, they'll stumble over their thoughts, interjecting "umm...," "like," "so," and a whole host of other words, and they'll repeat themselves.

Although dialogue doesn't have to ascribe to perfect naturalism, scenewriters can learn from these tendencies to vary the cadence and rhythm of their conversations. You can think of it as adding "artificial naturalism" so that the otherwise manufactured nature of your dialogue doesn't call attention to itself.

Consider the following. In this scene Pippa owns a flower shop. Lili is a middle schooler looking for a summer job:

```
                    PIPPA
          Do you have a resume? I'm not sure
          I can hire someone without any
          experience.

                    LILI
          This would be my first real job.
          But I had a paper route, and I mow
          my neighbor's lawn. Also, I love
          flowers, and I've helped my dad
          garden since I could carry a
          watering can.
```

Here, again, we have functional dialogue. It's a bit on the nose, but what's really notable is that these two characters let each other finish multi-sentence lines of dialogue. This is not to say that you can never have paragraphs in conversations. Only know that if you do, there should be a compelling narrative reason for it: one character is lecturing another, a character is giving a speech, making a long impassioned plea, or babbling on.

If your dialogue has multiple sentences per spoken line like this one, there's a quick and easy fix. Simply break up the lines and intersperse them:

```
              PIPPA
         Do you have a resume?

              LILI
         This would be my first real job.

              PIPPA
         I'm not sure I can hire someone
         without any experience.

              LILI
         But I had a paper route, and I mow
         my neighbor's lawn. Also, I love
         flowers, and I've helped my dad
         garden since I could hold a
         watering can.
```

This helps, but their grammatically perfect and complete sentences still sound stiff. Try reading them out loud. Who babbles nervously with perfect diction? What we can do is inject a few interruptions, pauses, and repetitions to create:

```
              PIPPA
         Do you have a resume?

              LILI
         This would be my first real job,
         but--

              PIPPA
         --I'm not sure I can hire someone
         without any experience.

              LILI
         I had a paper route--

              PIPPA
         This would be a little different.

              LILI
         Oh, and I mow my neighbor's lawn.
         Also, I, umm, love flowers, and,
         and, I've helped my dad garden
         since I could carry a watering
         can... Did I mention my paper
         route?
```

These interruptions fit both Pippa's impatience and Lili's nervousness. Lili's youth comes through clearly as she grasps for words in her desperate attempt to sound qualified. Her repetition underscores this and adds a bit of humor, too.

Check out the following dialogue excerpts. Consider how musicality and rhythm emerges from varying line and sentence length, pauses and interruptions, and repetitions.

From SCOTT PILGRIM VS. THE WORLD (page 39):

```
                    SCOTT
          Hey, can this not be a one night
          stand? For one thing, I didn't
          even get any...that was a joke.

                    RAMONA
          What did you have in mind?

                    SCOTT
          Umm...oh, come to the first round
          of this battle of the bands thing.

                    RAMONA
             (totally unimpressed)
          You have a band?

                    SCOTT
          Yeah, we're terrible. Please come.
```

In an exchange from QUEEN & SLIM (page 99), notice how the word "swear" is repeated, poetically, almost like a refrain:

```
                    SLIM
          If I do it will you please let me
          drive the rest of the way in
          peace?

                    QUEEN
          Swear to God.

                    SLIM
          Swear on something you believe in.

                    QUEEN
          Okay fine, I'll swear on you.
```

On page 37 of MOONLIGHT, Chiron is having dinner with Teresa. It's a dance between her questions and his statements, made poetic through repetitions of words like "good" and "call" and "say":

```
                    TERESA
          What's wrong?

                    CHIRON
          Nothing, I'm good.

                    TERESA
          Nah. I seen good and you ain't it:
          what's wrong, Little?

                    CHIRON
          Don't call me that.

                    TERESA
          Don't call you what? Your name?
          You grown now?

                    CHIRON
          I didn't say that.

                    TERESA
          Then what you sayin'?
```

EXERCISE: Music in Dialogue

This last exercise is about breathing musicality and contrast into your dialogue rather than changing its content.

Scan your scene dialogue to take note of every line that is more than one or two sentences. The longer any one character speaks, the more it feels like a lecture. Try interspersing these lines with ones that precede and/or follow it.

Go line by line and count the number of words—even syllables—you have in each. If your word/syllable count is relatively constant, vary the cadence to break things up.

Take a final pass where you have your characters interrupt each other, stumble over their thoughts, pause, and/or repeat themselves if it suits the situation. In other words, play with the language, tune it and tweak it with these naturalistic elements until you can hear the music in your dialogue.

12 Final Polish

Think of your scene as a guided tour you've put together for your readers. As the tour guide, you've curated a precise journey in order to give them a thrilling experience. You've deliberately ordered the stops, chosen landmarks that they absolutely must see, and directed their attention to details that will maximize the tour's entertainment value.

But before you guide your first customer, you might want to go over your tour one last time. Are you offering a majestic view of that waterfall? Are the roads well-maintained? Can we speed through that boring patch between the temple and the ruins? This chapter focuses on little adjustments you can make to ensure a captivating journey through your scene.

Once More with Feeling

You know that scene description exists to communicate to your reader pretty much everything that isn't communicated in dialogue. At a basic level, this means that it's used for character and location details and to chronicle specific actions and sounds that occur around them. Informational stuff, like: he picks the constable's pocket, or there's a loud explosion that catches everyone's attention, or she discovers a bear asleep in her bed.

But in addition to being functionally descriptive, scene description can be *evocative*. Consider a thief picking a pocket. The event itself needs to occur for your scene to continue, but what should it feel like? What tonal or emotional qualities would you like your readers to experience as they read it?

If it's your thief's first time picking a pocket, maybe there's danger and tension. If they've picked a thousand pockets before, the moment could feel as simple as drawing a breath. Or perhaps this is what your thief lives for, in which case the language could be layered with the thrills and joys of doing a thing they're great at.

Below we've pulled examples from four different scripts that showcase the evocative power of scene description.

Scene POV

Jojo first encounters Elsa, the Jewish girl hidden behind his sister's bedroom wall, on page 23 of JOJO RABBIT:

```
Then he sees a candle, bedding, a plate, a fork, AND...

...a SKINNY, PALE CREATURE hunched in the corner, its face
partially hidden beneath her hair, dark eyes staring back.

Screaming with fright, Jojo drops his knife and stumbles back
out into the room.
```

This is a wonderful example of scene description embodying a character's *point of view (POV)*. Note this term is distinct from a camera-specific POV where a shot looks like it was recorded through a character's eyes. When we say a scene is written from a particular character's point of view, we mean that the scene is built around that character's experience.

Waititi offers this first glimpse of Elsa from Jojo's POV. He uses the tropes of a horror film to drag out her reveal as a "creature" hiding in Jojo's house. The script will soon fill in details about Elsa as a scared, malnourished, and kind girl in hiding. But in this introduction she isn't even named. Instead Waititi takes his time describing the objects that define Elsa's world, mimicking Jojo's hesitation, curiosity, and fear to evoke the same fright that causes Jojo to run away.

Another example of a scene written from a specific point of view comes from LADY BIRD, when Kyle is seen on page 55 as if through Lady Bird's eyes:

```
Jenna joins Jonah & co in the parking lot, drinking and
smoking. Kyle is there, sitting on top of a car reading another
big book, a theoretical math book. For fun.
```

These lines direct the reader's attention with increasingly narrow focus. We get Kyle, we get his book, and then we get a close up of the book's subject. The words capture that feeling of walking up to someone and seeing more details as you get closer. Gerwig finishes with the snarky coda "for fun" to highlight what Lady Bird thinks.

Spotlight It

Another evocative piece of scene description appears when Jojo dances with his mother Rosie on page 44 of JOJO RABBIT:

```
Jojo laughs and gives in. He goes and dances with his mother.
Rosie holds her son close, squeezing him tightly, kissing him,
not letting go.
```

When you get down to the action of this scene, it's simply about Jojo dancing with his mom. But there is a subtext at play that Waititi underscores in his writing. One could easily overlook this as a lighthearted domestic moment, if not for Waititi's emphasis on Rosie's four (!) actions. That final line poetically and efficiently captures Rosie's love for her son, her desire to protect him and keep him close, and her knowledge that their time together is limited. She doesn't need to say all this stuff out loud; her love comes through her actions all the more palpably. Waititi shines a *spotlight* on the embrace, emphasizing its importance.

Another example of spotlighting a moment comes from page 10 of QUEEN & SLIM. When Queen and Slim are pulled over by a cop, Queen is incensed. Slim is trying to keep them alive:

```
                    SLIM
          I ain't tryna die tonight.

The weight of that statement leaps out of Slim's soul and lands
in Queen's lap.
```

By reflecting on Slim's line of dialogue with this powerful line of scene description, Waithe ensures that readers will not miss this young black man's justifiable mortal fear when confronted by a police officer. Sourced from his soul and given weight, his fear also builds a tangible connection between these first-time daters who haven't really found their connection yet. Without this spotlight to emphasize Slim's dialogue, what he says might pass as inconsequential or even a joke.

Writer's Commentary

Every now and then you might want to communicate something directly to your reader instead of writing it in the style of typical scene description. Staying with QUEEN & SLIM for a moment, let's take a look at how Waithe introduces the reader to Slim on page 6:

```
    Slim drives a WHITE HONDA ACCORD. Yeah, he don't give a fuck
    about cars. He tries to create a vibe by playing some neo-soul
    music. Which is regular soul music with a hint of patchouli.
```

Waithe's *commentary*, first about Slim's taste in cars and then his music, offers readers a quick (and funny) perspective to deepen our understanding of Slim. In other words, her commentary helps readers interpret the things that they're being shown, like: Slim doesn't drive a white Honda because it's safe, or it's what he can afford. He drives it because he doesn't care. The reader identifies with Slim (or laughs at, or with, him) through those interpretations. We might not all listen to neo-soul but, undoubtedly, we've all tried—and failed—to make an impression at one time or another.

We get another kind of commentary on page 16 of MOONLIGHT when Juan takes Little swimming for the first time:

```
    Juan and Little standing ashore, both of them pulling off their
    shoes, their shirts. This being Miami, both already dressed in
    shorts, this heat.
```

Instead of blandly pronouncing "it's hot" or having the characters discuss the heat, Jenkins lets readers feel the oppressive Miami sun in how the characters have dressed for it. The comment "this heat" is not coming from the characters but straight from Jenkins himself.

Poetic Impression

Another means of evoking emotion through scene description can be seen on page 82 of LADY BIRD. Here, Lady Bird and her mother Marion share a rare moment of joy:

> Marion and Lady Bird go to all the different open houses. They love doing this. They could never buy any of them, but it is so neat to see the inside of houses you've always known, and to imagine a different life. Where would your bed go?, etc. It's a great day. Maybe the best in a long time. Maybe ever.

We include this block of scene description with a caveat: it's not your typical scene description. It doesn't provide a blueprint for where to put the camera or what to show. But it is, without question, evocative. It points to what the moment is meant to do, even if it doesn't spell it all out.

This late in the script, readers know that money is an issue for Lady Bird's family. They know that Lady Bird lied about where she lived because she is embarrassed about her house. They know that Marion and Lady Bird do not get along, and they know that Lady Bird is upset about losing her virginity to Kyle. In other words, writer Greta Gerwig has already set up this powerful moment where Marion does something nice for her daughter right when Lady Bird needs a lift. The teen hyperbole at the end signals both how great this moment was and how fleeting it's likely to be.

Similarly, on page 74 of MOONLIGHT, writer Barry Jenkins introduces Jimmy's Eastside Diner:

> This is one of those relics that will always be a part of
> Miami. When the tide finally sweeps the city into the Atlantic,
> the last note rising from it will be Compay Segundo's "Chan
> Chan" reverberating from this place.

Even if you've never been to Miami or heard Segundo's hypnotic track, you can still feel the timelessness Jenkins evokes in this description. Notice how he doesn't bother with a single detail about countertops or coffee mugs. Whatever this diner looks like in your imagination comes from having your own idea of diners mashed-up with this Cuban-infused Miami flavor from Jenkins. There is plenty to draw from in imagining this location, and it's a beautiful way to involve the reader in the story.

EXERCISE: Write in the Feels

It's time to take a pass over your scene description with an eye towards squeezing the most feeling out of it.

Consider who your scene belongs to. Where is your character in their journey at this moment, and how does that information color their point of view of what's going on? Are they nervous and scared and therefore more likely to see the events going on through that lens? Are they feeling like the queen of the world, so they won't be flustered by anything? Choose a specific point of view and rewrite your scene description to capture it. In that revision, consider your choices of adjectives, verbs, and adverbs. Do they match the point of view you would like to express, or can you push your language more towards the extremes to evoke a clearer feeling for your reader?

Then, scan your scene for moments of scene description that fall flat or that fail to capture the full range of feelings that you intend. Enhance these weaker moments by shining a spotlight on important lines, adding commentary, and/ or using poetic descriptions.

Smooth It Out

English is a quirky language. After all, how is it possible that you can both "dust" a table with flour and "dust" a table to remove flour? Come on, dust, make up your mind! Are you making a mess or cleaning one up?

Regardless of the language you're writing in, you want to maximize your scene's readability. You have no control over whether a reader will skim your script, glance at it on a mobile phone between red lights, take it in while watching the news, or read it at all. But you do have control over what you give them, and you'll want to make the reading process as effortless as possible by avoiding a few common mistakes.

Eschew Impenetrability

Mark Twain is credited for saying "don't use a five-dollar word when a fifty-cent word will do." This is absolutely true for scenewriters. There is no benefit to using a fancy word that your reader may not understand if there's a perfectly good common word to substitute instead. You may think that big words make you look smart, but scenewriting is about clarity.

```
Kara approaches Janelle with élan. She reaches out to tap
Janelle on the shoulder when, suddenly, trepidation consumes
her and Kara retreats miserably.
```

The action of this moment should get the reader's heart racing. Kara is finally about to do something really nerve-wracking, but the lofty vocabulary of the description fails to convey that excitement.

Now consider the simple elegance of Lena Waithe's description to open QUEEN & SLIM:

```
INT. DINER - NIGHT 1 (SOMEWHERE IN OHIO)

We're in the kind of place that feels like everyone should know
your name. But they don't. Families frequent this spot when
they've fallen on hard times. It's practically empty on this
boring Thursday. SERVERS drop off hot plates while ELDERLY
PEOPLE sip cheap coffee at the counter.
```

Waithe's use of clear, common terms like "hard times," "boring Thursday," "hot plates," and "cheap coffee" builds a complex and rich picture of the diner without needing to overreach linguistically.

Avoid Ambiguity

When you use a word or sentence that can have multiple interpretations (like "dust"), you run the risk of confusing your reader. Don't make them work through ambiguities in order to puzzle out your intended meaning.

Homographs like "bow" (the verb) and "bow" (the noun) are words that are spelled the same but have different meanings. *Homophones* like "read" (the verb) and "reed" (the noun) are words that sound the same but have different meanings. English has dozens of each, and even some like "bank" and "fall" and "fly" that are both (*homonyms*).

Homographs require particular care; words like "object" and "tear" and "wind" are pronounced differently depending on their context. These words run the risk of not only tripping up your reader but anyone who might recite your dialogue out loud for the first time like, say, an actor at a live reading.

The following conversation has one intended interpretation. But because there are so many homographs, the meaning may be obscured on the first pass. If you're worried about misunderstanding and/or mispronouncing, it's best to clean something like this up before sharing it:

```
                    VASQUEZ
          I watched her perfect the dive,
          live, that exact minute. She's in
          the lead.

                    ELLE
          She fell like lead. I saw a flaw.
          Minute. But she'll live. It was
          near perfect.

                    DIVER
          I object! I'm a diver, not an
          object!
```

In addition to single word ambiguities like homographs, readers can easily stumble upon phrases or sentences if you don't write them carefully:

```
     Zach watched the kid with the binoculars.
```

Does Zach have the binoculars or does the kid?

```
                    ALIYAH
          Visiting relatives can be
          exhausting.
```

Is Aliyah talking about going to see her relatives, or relatives coming to visit?

SProoffrreading Are Important

If your draft comes in with no spelling or typographical errors, it would be a first in the history of writing. Nevertheless, an error-free scene is always an ideal worth striving for.

If a reader is looking for a reason to reject your script, misspelled and misused words are low-hanging fruit. They can make you look like you don't know what you're doing, and are precisely the kind of avoidable error that can disrupt a reader's experience of your content.

Take your time when you proofread. Look for spelling errors, misused and dropped words, and proofread for punctuation and grammar.

To be clear: spell-checking is NOT proofreading.

Yes, spell-checking will find any misspelled words and "fix" them, but as with homophones, a word that's spelled properly may still be used in error. The following would pass a computational spell-check but still contain some of the more common mistakes made in written English:

```
         Doug raced too the store and bought to many groceries.

                         SACHA
                 Their in there apartment, over
                 they're.

                         CHIOKO
                 Its not my fault it's breaks our
                 busted!
```

Here is the correct version:

```
         Doug raced to the store and bought too many groceries.

                         SACHA
                 They're in their apartment, over
                 there.

                         CHIOKO
                 It's not my fault its brakes are
                 busted!
```

Your goal in proofreading should be to correct these and other common mistakes. Make sure that your subject and verbs agree, that your tenses are consistent, that your pronouns refer to a specific noun, and know that, with joy in your heart, you can fully and freely embrace your love of a perfectly placed comma.

EXERCISE: Line by Line, for Clarity

Take a close and careful pass over your scene to eliminate anything that might interrupt your reader's experience. Go through your draft word by word looking for ambiguities, complicated word choices (when simpler ones would do), and errors (spelling, grammar, and misused words).

Every line of scene description should have one clear, intended meaning. If you find yourself working too hard to parse a given line, rewrite it with simpler word choices. Then rewrite it again to phrase your meaning in the clearest possible light.

Your screenwriting software should highlight misspelled words as you go. If you use new words unique to your story (unobtanium, lightsaber, MacGuffin), add them to the spellchecker's dictionary so that they stop being mislabeled as errors. Then, make sure that there are no misspellings or grammatical mistakes left anywhere in your scene.

Last Looks

The actual form of a piece of writing, and not just the content, greatly influences its reception. In other words, when a reader reads, their brain is taking in more than the words themselves. The look of what they're reading—things like font choice, spacing, and quality of the paper—are silently and powerfully playing a role.

Up until now, our primary focus throughout *SceneWriting* has been about what words will best help you tell your story. A last consideration, however, is how those words land visually on the page.

There are a few rigid elements that define the screenplay form: the font and colors are already set, the margins are preselected, and you will use sluglines, scene description, and dialogue to tell your story. Within those restrictions, however, there is an opportunity to explore the page graphically, to direct the reader's eye, to create emphasis, and continue to ensure that the reader's experience is carefree.

White Space for the Win

Given the page-per-minute convention of screenplays, you might think that a good way to shorten your script is to jam the text together into huge paragraphs. But it's not. When faced with a huge paragraph, readers actually have to work harder in order to keep track of where they are.

A script is a place where less is more. If you absolutely need all those lines of scene description, then don't stuff them into an unwelcoming block. Spread them out with line breaks.

Strive to minimize your blocks of scene description to a few sentences— between roughly one and three lines at a time—and separate those blocks with white space by inserting line breaks. Line breaks put a white frame around your most important points, highlighting them for your reader. And if you have a particular word that requires additional

emphasis

throw in line breaks before and after. For even more emphasis, you can add ALLCAPS, **bold**, or <u>underlining</u>. Using two of these in concert will definitely focus your reader on

SOMETHING SPECIFIC

if you really want to be sure that it won't get overlooked. However, just like we saw with allcaps in Chapter 7, it's easy to overdo it. Too much emphasis translates into no emphasis at all. If you

space

out

every

word

you are bound to leave readers wondering what's wrong with you.

Save extreme emphasis for the things that absolutely must be seen by your reader like those bits of visual information upon which your story hinges.

Thinking like a director, these are the moments when you might cut to a close up to reinforce a point. Scan a few scripts and you'll probably see isolated lines of scene description that illustrate this idea, such as:

```
the GUN

her crush, JANELLE

a CARD, hiding in the magician's shirt sleeve.
```

White space is important for dialogue, too. If a character is running at the mouth, break up their speech by inserting scene description or a wrylie. This has the added bonus of keeping your reader apprised of what's happening while the character is speaking.

BOOKSMART ends with Molly's graduation speech (page 99). It's not inordinately long, still the writers break it into smaller segments for easy reading:

```
                    MOLLY (CONT'D)
          You know, I was so...scared of you
          guys, I felt like I had to prove I
          was better than you. But really, I
          don't know any more than you. All
          I know is that we all have a lot
          more to learn.

Molly locks eyes with Amy. Amy smiles at her, emotional, proud.
All of a sudden Molly's about to cry.

                    MOLLY (CONT'D)
          Because this part's over. And
          that's so sad.

In the audience, Amy nods, tears in her eyes.

                    MOLLY (CONT'D)
          But it was great, wasn't it?
          Things are never going to be the
          same, but it was perfect.
                    (back to the audience)
          And I may not have before, but I
          see you. And you're great. Don't
          let college fuck it up.
                    (then)
          Congratulations, guys.
```

Compressing

The screenplay format gives you approximately 55 lines per page to work with, so do your best to make every one of those lines count. There is no reason to draw out banal moments with lots of detail. If a spy surreptitiously slips poison into our hero's drink at a bar, we're going to hang on every word that follows to see if she notices. The actions before (walking into the bar, finding a cozy spot to sit, and ordering a drink) are a prelude. They're setup. They may be essential to the scene, but they're unspectacular. They should be written so that the space they take on the page is proportional to the work they're doing in the story.

Compression is what we call the process of packing the necessary story information into a smaller space within the proper screenplay format. It's about getting each point across in the fewest number of lines possible so as to keep your scene moving apace.

To demonstrate this process, let's analyze the following quarter-page of screenplay text:

```
    Betty has finally had enough. She leaves her place at the back
    of the line and storms her way forward.

                        BETTY
                Hey--excuse me?

    The bouncer turns to her.

                        BETTY
                Hi. Look, I left my purse inside.
                Can you let me run in and grab it
                so I can get home?
```

This moment is clearly written, properly formatted, and gets the job done. It serves an important purpose in Betty's story since it's when she decides to confront the bouncer. It's a moment we're definitely going to keep in our scene, but let's take a shot at compressing it.

Since compression is all about line economy, take note that this block currently uses up 12 lines on the formatted page (blank lines are part of your line count).

We'll start by examining the first two lines, consisting of 20 words total:

```
Betty has finally had enough. She leaves her place at the back
of the line and storms her way forward.
```

The first step of compression is to translate the lines you have into beats. In this case, the beats can be summarized as:

A   Betty has had enough.

B   Betty is at the back of the line.

C   She leaves the line.

D   She storms forward.

Next let's determine if each of these beats are necessary. Beats that are redundant, beats that aren't providing new information, beats that are irrelevant, and beats where the information is implied elsewhere can generally be cut.

Beat A concerns the new information that Betty has lost her patience. It's a key change for Betty—one that's not communicated elsewhere—so we need to keep it.

Beat B tells the reader where Betty is in line. They may know this from earlier, but even if not, does it really matter if she's in the back? Beat A makes her location in line irrelevant since she's going to leave it anyway. We can safely cut beat B.

Beat C says that Betty leaves the line. Important, yes. But she can't storm forward in the next beat if she doesn't leave her spot. So D implies C. We can also safely cut C.

Cutting beats B and C leaves us with:

```
Betty has finally had enough. She storms her way forward.
```

These seem like the right two beats and we've already shortened our line count by one.

But before we move on, let's consider our word count and see if we can tighten these lines up any further. The current line is 10 words. Can we capture either of these ideas more succinctly? Absolutely! Consider:

```
Forget this. Betty storms forward.
```

We've gone from 20 words down to five, and from two lines down to one. The compressed action reads faster and packs a greater punch.

Moving on with our example, we have the following nine lines remaining:

```
                        BETTY
                Hey--excuse me?

        The BOUNCER turns to her.

                        BETTY
                Hi. Look, I left my purse inside.
                Can you let me run in and grab it
                so I can get home?
```

Let's again analyze the beats that comprise the section:

A Betty gets the bouncer's attention.

B She greets him.

C She says she left her purse inside.

D She asks to get it.

E She gives a reason for wanting it.

The new story information here is that Betty left her purse inside the club, she asks the bouncer for permission to reenter, and she wants her purse so she can get home. Beats A and B support the conversation but aren't adding new story information. And beat E is pretty clearly implied, if not irrelevant, so we can focus on preserving beats C and D.

Dialogue-wise, that looks like:

```
                    BETTY
          I left my purse inside. Can you
          let me run in and grab it?
```

Oops, we've overcompressed. We lost the introduction of the bouncer so we don't know who she is talking to anymore. Let's bring him back, but with greater efficiency.

Readers are following Betty. Is there an action she can take that will introduce the bouncer at this moment? She could tap him on the shoulder or wave at him, for example, which she'd probably have to do anyway since this is a busy outdoor scene.

Using this new idea along with some dialogue compression gives us:

```
                    BETTY
              (waves at the bouncer)
          Can I run in and grab my purse?
```

We've taken nine lines down to three.

Now let's focus on the tone. As it stands, Betty is brusque. Let's try another pass to make her more polite (which will translate into greater contrast if she goes ballistic later).

```
                        BETTY
                (waves to the bouncer)
            Sorry to bother you. Mind if I run
            in and grab my purse?
```

Here's the whole scene, post-compression:

```
    Forget this. Betty storms forward.

                        BETTY
                (waves at the bouncer)
            Sorry to bother you. Mind if I run
            in and grab my purse?
```

We've gone from 12 lines to six, and 51 words down to 23. That's a 50% reduction by both measures. Compressing at this rate will bring a bulky four page scene down to two pages.

There is no single, objective, best way to compress a moment. The point here is to show how a careful process of compression can tighten—and improve—scene description and dialogue throughout your scene.

EXERCISE: Expand and Compress

Time for your final exercise!

Start by scanning your fully formatted scene for big, uninterrupted blocks of scene description. Anything longer than three lines can be broken up with white space to give your important scene description room to breathe.

Next, look for key story elements in your scene description that should absolutely not be missed by your reader. If they're buried, consider using

new lines

to give them more emphasis.

Look for any long blocks of dialogue. Speeches that go on for more than a few lines can be divided up with wrylies or scene description. Consider showing the reader what else is happening in your scene at the same time.

Once you've spaced things out nicely, complete a full compression pass following the model introduced in this section. The mantra to follow is: "every line can be tightened, every line can be improved."

If you have a moment that runs two and a half lines, can you compress it down to two? Or, if it's merely setup, try to make it one. Compressing aggressively forces you to do a close reading of your work and ensure that every element in your scene is there for a reason.

Repeat this process of expanding and compressing until your scene converges on a form that's attractive on the page and efficient to read. Then go celebrate. You've done an outstanding job with your scene!

Okay, Now What?

Holy cow. You read the whole thing? Impressive.

You're ready to tackle your next scene, whether it's part of the same story you've been working on or another. Feel free to read through the book again verbatim or cherry-pick those ideas that you found most useful.

When you are feeling really good about your scene and/or your larger script, we've added a bonus chapter to give you some ideas on how to get the most out of sharing it.

If we're still allowed to give you homework this late in the game, it would be this: keep reading.

The more scripts you read, the more you will see great scenewriting in action. Whenever a moment moves you, stop and analyze how it works. Try to understand what the writer(s) did to have such a powerful impact on you and add their technique to your growing toolbox.

All that's left to say is: congratulations, scenewriter. We're looking forward to reading the amazing scripts you create!

Bonus Chapter: Expanding Your Development Circle

Throughout the book it's been you, yourself, and your scene. You've been crafting your writing so it leaps off the page for a hypothetical reader. But does it? There's only one way to find out: ask an actual reader.

For new scenewriters in particular, it can be extremely valuable to learn how readers respond to your smaller scene before you commit a ton of time and energy to fleshing out a longer script. Are your choices eliciting the responses you hoped for? Does the story make sense? Are you getting the most out of the fact that this is a screenplay and not, say, a short story?

When to share your writing depends on what you want to get out of the experience. If you've been around the block a few times and feel confident in your command of the fundamentals, then you may choose to wait and share your work only after you've finished a full script. But if you're new to writing, you may want to run things by a friendly reader in the early stages.

Whatever path you choose, it takes courage to share your work, and some thoughtful planning will help you get the most out of the process. Writing is meant to be read, and when you're ready to get some eyes on it, the potential rewards are many, both for your scene and for your overall growth as a writer.

Not All Readers Are Created Equal

You might think it's time to reach out to your second cousin's partner who's a creative exec at Disney. Or that guy your sister dated whose college roommate is Shonda Rhimes's personal assistant.

Before you do: don't.

Not yet. Assuming this is your first time working through *SceneWriting*, you are sitting on a gorgeous, polished draft of a single scene, but it's also one that has never seen the light of day. If you have a tenuous link to a powerful industry dealmaker, or a connection who can get you to one, wait until you have a bullet-proof full script before reaching out to them. You may only get one chance, so you'll want to make the most of it.

In the meantime, if you'd like to get some feedback on what you've written, there are plenty of other options. Non-industry folks, friends, and other developing scenewriters can be wonderful sources of critique; after all, these are the very kinds of people you want to draw in by the millions when the final produced version of your script is presented.

As you consider recruiting readers from your various circles, one quality that's paramount is a person's *willingness* to read your writing. A willing reader is a great reader, period. With the right preparation, anyone willing to share their opinion can be useful. An unwilling reader, well, what's the point? The last thing you want is feedback from someone who felt obliged to give it.

You may not realize it yet, but your circles are filled with willing readers. Take your loved ones as a starting point. They (hopefully) support you and want to see you succeed, and would likely be excited to spend a few minutes with your scene if they know how much it might help you. But there are also work colleagues, classmates, neighbors, teachers, bartenders; your world is full of people who love TV and movies, and that's really what you're looking for here.

There is a second quality to consider beyond willingness, and that is your reader's level of screenwriting knowledge. A willing reader can give personal reactions, but a willing reader with some craft knowledge can also suggest actionable changes. Craft-aware readers have all attempted the same thing you're doing. The specifics of your scene are different, but the challenge is the same.

EXERCISE: Build Your Reading Roster

Go through your various contacts and consider who you might be able to recruit to read your work. Start with those people you are most comfortable asking, then broaden your search. Think about family, friends, classmates, workmates, or acquaintances with a background in the arts. Write down the names of anyone you think might be happy to help out, and put a star next to anyone who has even a hint of screenwriting experience.

If anyone on your list qualifies as an "influential industry professional," put a box around their name and save them for the future unless they have already signaled to you that they would like to mentor you in your career. If they haven't, it's best to save those contacts for when your work has been vetted and you feel confident about its standing.

You may not identify any screenwriters in your circle at all. If that's where you find yourself, look for a writing group to connect with. It's great if you can find a group of dedicated screenwriters, but even a general writing group with playwrights, novelists, poets, or other writers would be a solid start. These are people committed to learning craft, just like you. What you're looking for is a forum that allows you to share your work and receive feedback from the other members. Joining a writing group will also give you exposure to other people's writing. This can provide a forum to offer critique, and you'll get to see other people's creative choices in action. Watching and learning from other writers as they transform their work through revisions can be enormously instructive.

Head down to your local bookstore or café to see if anyone has posted a flyer for a writing group. You can also try searching online (but not all groups advertise themselves). If you're at a school, ask fellow students and teachers if there are any groups that you might join. Many companies, as well, have groups that get together outside of work hours to share and workshop writing. If you really can't find anyone, try putting up flyers or leveraging social media. Give yourself a goal to find just one other up-and-coming screenwriter who you can learn and grow with.

Readings Are Fundamental

There are two different ways of sharing your work: you can give someone your work to read on their own, or you can organize a real-time table reading. Both have their strengths and weaknesses.

Individual private readings are generally the easiest to make happen because they can occur on the reader's schedule. Of course, this also means that your reader might end up skimming your scene while arguing with their kids, cooking dinner, or watching the nightly news. Or not reading it at all. On the other hand, they might lock the door, put on noise-cancelling headphones, and fully immerse themselves in your work. The problem is, you can't be sure.

Group readings guarantee that your work gets heard, but they require planning. You will need to reserve a comfortable space, find a group of willing participants, and make sure everyone has a copy of your work to read and knows which character(s) they're reading. If you want to cast real actors, you'll need to do that well in advance (we recommend reaching out to local schools and theater groups for candidates).

But the benefits of hearing your work read aloud are many. Without question, you will learn new things about your script every time you hear it. Repeated words will stand out, awkward dialogue will become clear, typos and ambiguities will be found, and some lines that you've read a hundred times might sound confusing. You will also be able to tell from the vibe of the room if a moment is working or falling flat.

During such readings, keep one eye on the script and another on the participants. It's good to take note of reactions as they occur, but it can be difficult to concentrate on multiple things at once. If you can get the permission of your participants, record the reading so you can digest their comments and reactions later.

When you're ready to draft an invitation to one or more willing readers on your roster, let them know exactly what they're in for. Be clear about how many pages you're covering, what genre you're working in, and how long you expect the event to take. For example: "My script is a three-page scene from a horror film. It should take about half an hour for the reading and discussion."

It's also a good idea to give the group a heads-up about what kind of feedback you're seeking (more on that below). By giving potential readers an honest introduction, you are allowing them to politely say, "Wow, I'm really just not a horror person," or "I've got a busy week," and save you the struggle of trying to wrestle feedback from an unwilling participant.

First-Time Readers

At this stage of your writing process, it's important to keep in mind that first-time readers are a particularly special gift. They don't know what you're trying to do and therefore must glean everything from what appears on the page. If a first-time reader doesn't "get" something, it's probably because that thing has not been clearly communicated in your script (it's underwritten). On the other hand, if a first-time reader has a strong emotional or intellectual reaction, you can trust that your writing is firing on all cylinders.

Repeat readers are wonderful too, but they'll be informed by prior exposure to your script. Because of this dynamic, it's useful to have at least one set of fresh eyes on every draft. This requires restraint—if you give your first "final" draft to everyone on your list right away, then you'll have no first-time readers for your next iteration. So keep a few willing participants in reserve for subsequent reads.

Slings and Arrows

You're sharing your work with readers for one reason: to make it better. You've done the best you could on your own and now you need their help to see where your scene is working and where it isn't. By design, therefore, any reading process is going to expose you and your script to critique.

There is an art to soliciting and receiving critique. When you do it right, you can get a ton of invaluable input to improve your work. But if you're not prepared, you can end up lost in a jungle of feedback or depressed about the state of your writing. Or both.

Before any kind of reading, it's important to let your readers know what kind of feedback would be most helpful. Are you looking for a pat on the back, or general impressions, or a thorough vetting of your scene? Whatever you want, make it clear from the outset. The more transparent you can be with yourself and your readers, the better.

Prepping Questions

Prepare a list of questions about the script that you would like your readers to consider. When doing so, avoid "feel" questions. Instead of "do you feel there is a clear and satisfying resolution?" ask "What is the resolution?" or "What action marks the end of the scene for you?" Targeted questions will direct a reader's critique towards the core of what you're trying to accomplish. Here are some examples of other targeted questions:

What does the main character want?

Why do they want it?

What is the most engaging/exciting part of the scene for you?

Did you lose interest at any point during the scene? If so, when?

What do you anticipate will happen in the next scene?

Were you confused about the action at any moment?

In *x* line of dialogue is it clear that the character is talking about *y*?

What films or shows do you consider comparable to this one?

Note that none of these questions refer to "my" scene or "my" characters or "my" story. This may be subtle, but by disassociating yourself from the scene you prime your readers to critique the work, not the creator. This also leaves them room to have their own experience with the world and characters. Parsing a comment like, "Wow, Betty sure reminds me of my sister!" can lead to a fruitful conversation about what is (or isn't) coming across about Betty.

Taste-driven questions won't be directly helpful to your revision process. Avoid questions such as those below:

Did you like it?

Do you think character *x* is cool?

Was it too short, or too long?

Did you have a favorite part?

Yes/no questions like these don't invite elaboration. Consider the following yes/no question: "Would you want to continue reading based on this scene?" On the surface it seems like a pretty great question since it gets right to the core of engagement, namely, does someone find the work compelling enough to want to continue? If you hear "yes" then you feel pretty good. But if the answer is "no," then you're out of luck. You have no further data to help you diagnose and fix whatever is wrong.

Even if you ask "why?" after a question like that, you still may not get the feedback you need. A response like: "I don't know, it's really just not my thing" doesn't give you a lot to work with.

You'll likely prepare different questions for different readers and/or readings. On a reading of your first draft, for example, you might be very interested in finding out if your plot details are clear. In a later read, you may be more focused on tone and engagement. If your reader is a scenewriting craft-nerd like you, then you can include craft-specific questions that wouldn't make sense for a general audience like, "Would you cut the fourth wryly and put the action into scene description?" and "Is the resolution of my treasure hunt clear?"

Receiving Critique

When you're actually receiving feedback from readers, your job is to listen to what they have to say, ask for clarification if you need it, and appreciate them for engaging with your work. That's all. If they start listing comparable films or shows (comps) that feel way off-base to you, write them down and smile. If they report that your action sequence dragged, or that the dialogue sounded unrealistic, note it and thank them.

You're there to get information, not to engage in a debate with your volunteer readers. In fact, the more time your readers are talking (and you're not) the better. Don't waste time justifying or defending your choices. Instead, listen and understand the critique. Get everything you can from the reading while it's happening. And the fact of the matter is, either the readers got what you were trying to do or they didn't. If the latter, then you need to learn how and where it failed for them.

In the rare instances when participants substitute their own agenda for answering your questions, there's not much to do beyond toughing it out and thanking them for their input.

Lastly, be aware of the time and honor your schedule. End the reading when it's supposed to end. And when you're done getting feedback from an individual or from a group, be sure to thank everyone for the time and attention they devoted to your project. By approaching your work in a professional, responsible, and respectful way like this, you will make sure they see you as the considerate and reliable person you are.

EXERCISE: Preparing for a Reading

There is a lot of "writing that supports the writing" in the life of a scenewriter. In addition to your script, you can end up drafting loglines, pitch bibles, summaries, query letters, emails and more to help get your project into the right hands.

This exercise gets you started down that path by drafting brief introductory remarks and a set of targeted questions tailored to get the most out of your reading.

Introductory materials are useful for both individual and group reading situations. They help position the reader(s) in the right frame of mind and set their expectations. You might wonder: why bother with introductory materials at all? Doesn't the scene speak for itself? Yes, it does, but setting up your material briefly and clearly will help avoid awkward situations like a reader signing up to read a comedy only to discover it's a psycho-thriller instead.

With this context-setting in mind, write a brief one- to three-sentence introduction to your material so that your reader can decide if and when they're ready to spend time with it. Focus on tone and genre rather than story specifics: "It's a laugh-out-loud romp through high school" or "it's a dark study of human nature after the apocalypse" would work better than "it's a story about a girl and her cat." For example, THE LORD OF THE RINGS is a gripping fantasy action/adventure, not a story about destroying jewelry.

Next, write down all the questions you're thinking of asking your readers about your work. Start by brainstorming everything that you might like to know about your script, then consider your questions more tactically (per the discussion above). Rewrite the questions that will actually be most helpful to you, bearing in mind that they should be open-ended (not yes/no) and specific to the story elements you'd like to discuss. When you ultimately bring questions to your readers, keep the count reasonable (like three to five in total) so as not to overwhelm them. The questions you pose should be easy to understand and easy to answer.

Found in Translation

Each reading is going to give you valuable data on how your scene plays in the minds of real readers. But how do you integrate that input into your next revision? If someone was confused by a part of your scene, do you dive right in and try to clarify the confusing part? What if others really liked that part but were instead bothered by something else?

You have worked hard to engineer an engaging and informative script. Even if it's not working perfectly yet, you have a lot of interconnected parts that play off each other. To revise or pull a chunk out of your scene may indeed be the right fix, but it also may bring the whole thing down like a tower of Jenga blocks. Therefore, when it comes to acting on your feedback, we encourage a four-step process to make sure you're making the right changes for the right reasons.

Collecting

The first thing you'll want to do is collect all the feedback you received. It's important that you have the comments AND that you understand those comments. This might sound silly, but we've come home from readings with shorthand notes scribbled hastily onto the margins of a scene like:

> Too angry. Dalmatians.

The words are clear, but what the heck does this note mean? The good news is that if you act quickly and review your notes soon after your reading, you're likely to remember that your shorthand actually meant:

> Carol felt that Betty sounded too angry here. She reminded her of Cruella de Vil from ONE HUNDRED AND ONE DALMATIANS.

If you have a recording of the verbal feedback you received, you should go through it and transcribe the important parts into text. This will make the comments easier to find and organize as you work on them later.

Even if you receive written feedback, it's helpful to go over it immediately and make sure that you understand all of the points. If not, ask for clarification on any items that don't make sense.

Waiting

This can be hard, but it's probably the most important thing you can do for your relationship to your work. Put your scene in a drawer for a week. Seriously. Try and forget that you wrote a scene and that you are super eager to revise it. Do other things. Live your life. Read, talk, cook, play.

Waiting does two things for you. First, and most importantly, it allows you to see your work with fresh eyes. The longer you can be apart from your scene, the more you will be able to see its strengths and weaknesses the next time you read it. Believe it or not, you will one day have the shocking experience of reading something that *you completely forgot that you wrote*. You'll be impressed with yourself ("Wow, this is pretty good!"), but you'll also see easy fixes that you simply weren't able to see earlier. This is the power of distance.

The second thing that waiting does is minimize any lingering emotional attachments you have to the feedback you received live. This objective distance is necessary to allow you to make revisions based on what's best for the scene and not your ego. It might have been hard to hear that your main character isn't likeable, for example, but after a week you can stop taking it personally and focus on what the comments really suggest.

Translating

Translating feedback into actionable items can be a real challenge.

For example, someone says your character sounds too angry in a specific line of dialogue. What do they mean by "too angry"? Too angry for the tone you had established? Too angry for the personality of the character? Too angry given the situation?

What matters most is that this line of dialogue disrupted a reader and took them out of your scene. You need to understand why. It might be that the line's wrong, the context is wrong, or that the reader missed something or doesn't realize where you're going.

If you hear your character's not "likeable," it probably means the reader doesn't understand the relatable qualities of their goal. If you hear that something is "boring," check to see if the conflict and stakes and approach are all clear. If you hear that a line of dialogue sounds "unrealistic" or "forced," check to see if your exposition is obvious. Look to translate the various red flags from your readers into things you can directly change.

Nearly every comment you receive can be translated into a point about one of the fundamental scene elements—character goal, motivation, obstacle, and approach (see Part I)—or the delivery of one of these elements (see Parts II and III). These are the building blocks of your scene, the expression of your main character's journey, and if they aren't clear and engaging to a reader, it will cause confusion or boredom.

You might also decide that you disagree with a note. That's perfectly fine too. You are the author and you have final say. Perhaps a display of anger is important to your character's development, and comes back in a later scene. Maybe you deliberately want to call attention to this character's short fuse. Regardless, it is perfectly fine to translate a note into the actionable item of: "leave as is," or "get more feedback first."

Look for trends in the comments you receive. Single observations may emerge from one reader's specific tastes, interpretation, or misinterpretation, but when multiple people point to an issue with the same moment, it's probably less about taste and more about an inconsistency or disruption in your scene.

Revising

Only after you have clearly understood the notes, have given them time to sit, and have turned them into a list of actionable items, should you dive in and revise. As always, duplicate your scene. Then walk through your to-do list and make it incrementally better, like you have been doing throughout Part III.

EXERCISE: Lather, Rinse, Repeat

You are ready to share your work with others, solicit their feedback, and integrate those comments into subsequent revisions. Go for it! Reach out to a few people on your list and see who is willing to read your scene. Look for a writing group critique session at school or at work. Get your scene out there so that you can begin to see how your writing is received. Use the materials you generated earlier in this chapter to frame your scene for the readers and to get the most useful feedback you can from them.

When you feel like you've got enough material to merit one, arrange a table reading. It's fun and incredibly valuable to hear your words come from the mouths of trained actors. It's a great way to meet other people interested in writing and to begin to build contacts. Always be kind. Make sure you're respectful of your readers' time and energy, and you'll soon build up a network that will help you take your scenewriting to the next level.

Use the feedback you receive to iterate over your script and make it as perfect as it can be.

Appendix A: References

Below are all the scripts quoted directly in *SceneWriting*.

AMERICAN BEAUTY	Alan Ball	1999
ARRIVAL	Eric Heisserer	2016
BOOKSMART	Emily Halpern & Sarah Haskins and Susanna Fogel and Katie Silberman	2019
CAN YOU EVER FORGIVE ME?	Nicole Holofcener and Jeff Whitty	2018
DIRK GENTLY	Max Landis	2010
DO THE RIGHT THING	Spike Lee	1989
EIGHTH GRADE	Bo Burnham	2018
GET OUT	Jordan Peele	2017
JOJO RABBIT	Taika Waititi	2019
KIDDING	Series created by Dave Holstein	2018
LADY BIRD	Greta Gerwig	2017
LITTLE MISS SUNSHINE	Michael Arndt	2006
MANCHESTER BY THE SEA	Kenneth Lonergan	2016
MOONLIGHT	Barry Jenkins	2016
MOONRISE KINGDOM	Wes Anderson and Roman Coppola	2012
PARASITE	Bong Joon Ho and Han Jin Won	2019
QUEEN & SLIM	Lena Waithe	2019
SCOTT PILGRIM VS. THE WORLD	Edgar Wright & Michael Bacall	2010
SELMA	Paul Webb and Ava DuVernay	2014
THE INCREDIBLES	Brad Bird	2004
THE WAY WAY BACK	Nat Faxon and Jim Rash	2013
THE WIRE	David Simon	2002
WALL-E	Andrew Stanton, Jim Reardon	2008
WHEN HARRY MET SALLY	Nora Ephron	1989

Here is a list of every other film, book, and show mentioned but not directly cited in the text.

12 YEARS A SLAVE	John Ridley	2013
2001	Stanley Kubrick and Arthur C. Clarke	1968
ALL IS LOST	J. C. Chandor	2013
ALL THE PRESIDENT'S MEN	William Goldman	1976
AVATAR: THE LAST AIRBENDER	Series created by Michael Dante DiMartino and Bryan Konietzko	2005
AVENGERS: INFINITY WAR	Christopher Markus and Stephen McFeely	2018
BALLERS	Series created by Stephen Levinson	2015
BRIDESMAIDS	Kristen Wiig and Annie Mumolo	2011
CASABLANCA	Julius J. Epstein, Philip G. Epstein, and Howard Koch	1942
CASTAWAY	William Broyles Jr.	2000
CHERNOBYL	Craig Mazin	2019
CROUCHING TIGER, HIDDEN DRAGON	Hui-Ling Wang, James Schamus, and Kuo Jung Tsai	2000
CSI: MIAMI	Series created by Ann Donahue, Carol Mendelsohn, and Anthony E. Zuiker	2002
DIE HARD	Jeb Stuart and Steven E. de Souza	1988
DISTRICT 9	Neill Blomkamp and Terri Tatchell	2009
DOWNSIZING	Alexander Payne and Jim Taylor	2017
ERIN BROCKOVICH	Susannah Grant	2000
EX MACHINA	Alex Garland	2014
FINDING NEMO	Andrew Stanton, Bob Peterson, and David Reynolds	2003
GAME OF THRONES	Series created by David Benioff and D. B. Weiss	2011

GRAVITY	Alfonso Cuarón and Jonás Cuarón	2013
GROUNDHOG DAY	Danny Rubin and Harold Ramis	1993
HEATHERS	Daniel Waters	1989
HOWL'S MOVING CASTLE	Hayao Miyazaki	2004
INTO THE WILD	Sean Penn	2007
ISN'T IT ROMANTIC	Erin Carillo, Dana Fox, and Katie Silberman	2019
JAWS	Peter Benchley and Carl Gottlieb	1975
MIAMI VICE	Series created by Anthony Yerkovich	1984
MONTY PYTHON AND THE HOLY GRAIL	Graham Chapman, John Cleese, Eric Idle, Terry Gilliam, Terry Jones, and Michael Palin	1975
MOUSEHUNT	Adam Rifkin	1997
NATIONAL TREASURE	Jim Kouf, Cormac Wibberley, and Marianne Wibberley	2004
NO COUNTRY FOR OLD MEN	Joel Coen and Ethan Coen	2007
NORTH BY NORTHWEST	Ernest Lehman	1959
ONE HUNDRED AND ONE DALMATIANS	Bill Peet and Dodie Smith	1961
PEN15	Series created by Maya Erskine, Anna Konkle, and Sam Zvibleman	2019
PRINCESS MONONOKE	Hayao Miyazaki	1997
RAIDERS OF THE LOST ARK	Lawrence Kasdan	1981
RICK AND MORTY	Series created by Dan Harmon and Justin Roiland	2013
SAVING PRIVATE RYAN	Robert Rodat	1998
SCARFACE	Oliver Stone	1983
SEX EDUCATION	Series created by Laurie Nunn	2019
SOUTH PARK	Series created by Trey Parker, Matt Stone, and Brian Graden	1997

SPIDER-MAN: INTO THE SPIDERVERSE	Phil Lord and Rodney Rothman	2018
STAR WARS	George Lucas	1977
SULLIVAN'S TRAVELS	Preston Sturges	1941
THE BABADOOK	Jennifer Kent	2014
THE BAD NEWS BEARS	Bill Lancaster	1976
THE CHRONICLES OF NARNIA: THE LION, THE WITCH AND THE WARDROBE	Ann Peacock and Andrew Adamson and Christopher Markus & Stephen McFeely	2005
THE DRIVER	Walter Hill	1978
THE HANDMAID'S TALE	Series created by Bruce Miller	2017
THE HOBBIT	J. R. R. Tolkien	1937
THE KING'S SPEECH	David Seidler	2010
THE LORD OF THE RINGS	J. R. R. Tolkien	1954
THE LORD OF THE RINGS: THE FELLOWSHIP OF THE RING	Fran Walsh & Philippa Boyens & Peter Jackson	2001
THE LORD OF THE RINGS: THE RETURN OF THE KING	Fran Walsh & Philippa Boyens & Peter Jackson	2003
THE MARTIAN	Drew Goddard	2015
THE MATRIX	Lilly Wachowski & Lana Wachowski	1999
THE NAKED GUN: FROM THE FILES OF POLICE SQUAD!	Jerry Zucker & Jim Abrahams & David Zucker & Pat Proft	1988
THE PRINCESS BRIDE	William Goldman	1987
THE ROAD	Joe Penhall	2009
THE SHAWSHANK REDEMPTION	Frank Darabont	1994
THE SILENCE OF THE LAMBS	Ted Tally	1991
THE SIMPSONS	Series created by Matt Groening	1989
THE SOCIAL NETWORK	Aaron Sorkin	2010
THE SURE THING	Steve Bloom and Jonathan Roberts	1985

THE TERMINATOR	James Cameron and Gale Anne Hurd	1984
THE WIZARD OF OZ	Noel Langley & Florence Ryerson and Edgar Allan Woolf	1939
TOUCH OF EVIL	Orson Welles	1958
TOY STORY 2	Andrew Stanton and Rita Hsian and Doug Chamberlin & Chris Webb	1999
WESTWORLD	Series created by Jonathan Nolan and Lisa Joy	2016
ZOOTOPIA	Jared Bush & Phil Johnston	2016

Appendix B: Course Adoption Guide

SceneWriting can serve as the primary text for a course on writing scenes, or it can be easily integrated (in whole or in part) as supporting material into screenwriting classes at all levels. Below we explore these options in detail.

A Scenewriting-Only Course

This full-credit course is designed so that each student produces two fully realized scenes over a 14-week semester. Taking a deep dive into the craft of scenewriting empowers students to produce stronger scenes for shorts, series, or features. Students work their way through the entire *SceneWriting* text, completing every exercise to put theoretical material into practice. They also read one published script per week, chosen from Appendix A or elsewhere. This syllabus assumes approximately three in-class contact hours per week and four hours of student work outside of class.

Week 1: Character Goal, Motivation, and Obstacle

Read *SceneWriting* Chapters 1 and 2 and do all exercises.

Read a published feature or series script.

Week 2: Character Approach and Setting

Read *SceneWriting* Chapters 3 and 4 and do all exercises.

Read a published feature or series script.

Week 3: Scene Description, Dialogue, and Reader Engagement

Read *SceneWriting* Chapters 5 and 6 and do all exercises.

Read a published feature or series script.

Week 4: Drafts

Read *SceneWriting* Chapters 7 and 8 and do all exercises.

Read a published feature or series script.

Week 5: Scene Length and Obvious Exposition

Read *SceneWriting* Chapters 9 and 10 and do all exercises.

Read a published feature or series script.

Week 6: Authentic Dialogue and Final Polish

Read *SceneWriting* Chapters 11 and 12 and do all exercises.

Read a published feature or series script.

Weeks 7–8: In-Class Table Readings

Read *SceneWriting* Chapter 13 and do all exercises.

Read two published feature or series scripts.

Weeks 9–12: New Scenes

Develop 6–10 new pages of work following the *SceneWriting* method.

Read four more published feature or series scripts.

Weeks 13–14: Final In-Class Table Readings of New Work

Gather and incorporate feedback from readings into final revisions.

Custom Modular Adoption

The structure of the book makes it easy to pick readings and exercises to supplement any existing screenwriting course. Since every course is different, educators are encouraged to cherry-pick the chapters and sections of *SceneWriting* that they feel offer their students the most valuable information to complement their existing syllabi.

Educators seeking material about story planning (character goal, motivation, obstacle, approach, theme, and setting) should draw from Part I. This is particularly useful for courses that develop beat sheets or treatments.

Educators seeking material about script drafting (basics of scene description and dialogue, maximizing reader engagement, and formatting) should draw from Part II. This is particularly useful for courses that include writing a full draft.

Educators seeking material about revision (scene length, hiding exposition, authentic dialogue, final polish, and receiving feedback) should draw from Part III. This is particularly useful for courses that focus on revising.

Below we propose several ways of incorporating a *SceneWriting* module into common screenwriting curricula.

Example Adoption into a Pilot- or Feature-Writing Course

Screenwriting courses that are designed to help students develop a pilot or feature project usually culminate in a treatment or a first draft. To best support the writing of that end product, we encourage adding a *SceneWriting*-based module before the drafting phase, based on how much time there is available, as follows:

One week for *SceneWriting*:

Read the whole book, skipping the exercises.

Two weeks for *SceneWriting*:

Read the whole book.

If students are writing a treatment, they should complete the exercises in Chapter 3 for every scene in their outline or beat sheet.

If students are writing a full first draft, they should complete the exercises in Chapters 7 and 8 for every scene in their script.

If the course also includes a module on revision, then we encourage incorporating chapters and exercises from Part III. The more time students can spend on revisions the better. Here are two options for including a module on revisions:

One day:

After a first draft is complete, read Part III to prepare for revisions (but skip the exercises).

One or more weeks:

After a first draft is complete, read Part III to prepare for revisions. Complete the exercises in Chapters 9, 10, 11, and 12 for as many scenes from the script as possible.

Example Adoption into a Short Film Writing Course

In courses where the aim is to complete a script shorter than a feature or pilot, there is often more time available for students to plan, draft, and perfect their work. Below are two possible adoption strategies for incorporating *SceneWriting* into such a course:

One week:

Read Parts I and II before embarking on the first draft, skipping the exercises.

Read Part III after writing the first draft, skipping the exercises.

Two or more weeks:

Read Parts I and II before embarking on the first draft. Do the exercises in Chapters 7 and 8 for every scene in the script.

Read Part III after writing the first draft. Complete the exercises in Chapters 9, 10, 11, and 12 for every scene in the script.

Acknowledgments

We would like to begin by thanking Noah Schwartzberg, Acquisitions Editor at Fairchild Books, for introducing us to the astute and remarkably supportive Katie Gallof at Bloomsbury. This book wouldn't exist if not for her patience, guidance, diligence, and wisdom. Thank you, Katie! We'd also like to thank the amazing team of Merv Honeywood, Juliet Gardner, Eleanor Rose, and Jonathan Nash for their extraordinary support of our vision for the printed book.

We would like to recognize Hampshire College as the incredibly special institution that it is—truly the most innovative college out there, a wonderful school to attend, and a fantastic place to teach. Hopping into the way-back machine, we owe a debt of gratitude to Dean Steve Weisler who green-lit the first class we co-taught in short film development—hope you are enjoying kangaroo chops out west, Steve.

What makes Hampshire so special are the unique individuals it attracts, including so many of our students who have made us better writers and teachers. In particular, we are grateful to Bill Bowles and Kevin Cline for bravely joining forces with us on the mad dash to TRIVIAL PURSUITS; Aaron Edell, Steve Gifford, and Tim O'Neill for bringing their intelligence, humor, and writing talents to the Screenwriting Workshop; and Connie Chang, Tim Childs, Dutch Clark, Ally McCarthy, Jordan Miron, and Max Simonet for showing how bright, progressive, and irreverent the future of writing will be.

We have been so fortunate to collaborate and discuss writing with talented colleagues like Chris Bishop, Jake Blais, Julie Galdieri, Dan Gilbert, Oren Jacob, Marlo Hunter, Daniel Kramer, Jacob Lefton, Michael Marantz, Zach MacDonald, James McGuire, Ian Morgan, Phi Phi Anh Nguyen, Jason Oppliger, Lydia Parker, Donald Sanders, Kimberly Senior, Todd Shifflett, and Evan Viera.

Eric would like to acknowledge a huge debt of gratitude to the brilliant, kind, and urbane James Schamus for offering a first foray into the professional film world. Getting to listen in on conversations at Good Machine and seeing the intelligence of Schamus, Ang Lee, and Ted Hope on display was the spark that ignited a lifetime love of understanding how film and scripts work. He would also like to thank the late director Michael H. Shamberg for the practical and unforgettable experience of working on location in Paris and New York. Finally, thanks to Chris for all the many years of collaboration, from co-teaching to writing, producing, directing, and editing films together. It's been quite a journey since Amherst.

Chris would like to thank Will Reiser for inviting him into multiple rewarding screenwriting collaborations and sharing countless informal yet deeply impactful craft lessons along the way; Taj Musco, Jericca Cleland, Dan Attias, and Susan Shilliday for leveraging their own talents and advice in support of his writing career; and Michael Schurter for many years of a productive, hilarious, and therapeutic writing partnership. Oh, and Eric. Chris would like to thank Eric for willingly and eagerly joining forces when we finally stopped saying, "We should write a book about that," and decided to actually do it.

The following educational resources have been instrumental to our own learning and teaching: the long-running Scriptnotes podcast from John August and Craig Mazin, *The Screenwriter's Bible* by David Trottier, *Backwards & Forwards* by David Ball, *The Coffee Break Screenwriter* by Pilar Alessandra, *Making a Good Script Great* by Linda Seger, *In the Blink of an Eye* by Walter Murch, *Story* by Robert McKee, *Save The Cat* by Blake Snyder, *The Screenwriter's Workbook* by Syd Field, and multiple WGA-sponsored story webinars by Jacob Krueger.

Lastly and most importantly, we'd like to offer thanks to our parents, siblings, and to Lise, Viveca, Henry, Jordy, and Noe, for supporting us as writers and teachers both.

Index

www.ingramcontent.com/pod-product-compliance
Ingram Content Group UK Ltd.
Pitfield, Milton Keynes, MK11 3LW, UK
UKHW020738280225
455688UK00012B/721